my tiny
garden

my tiny
garden

STYLISH IDEAS FOR SMALL SPACES

Lucy Anna Scott with **Lucy Conochie**
Photography by Jon Cardwell

PAVILION

First published in the United Kingdom in 2016 by
Pavilion
1 Gower Street
London
WC1E 6HD

ISBN 978-1-91049-654-1

A CIP catalogue record for this book is available from the British Library.

10 9 8 7 6 5 4 3 2 1

Reproduction by Mission, Hong Kong
Printed and bound by Toppan Leefung Printing Ltd, China

This book can be ordered direct from the publisher at www.pavilionbooks.com

Lucy, Jon and Lucy would like to thank all of the inspirational gardeners who took part in the making of this book. Each of you has given us so much. Thank you for allowing us into your homes, for your hospitality, for the tea and pastries, for the Meyer lemons, for the making of last-minute arrangements and for all the last-minute lifts to the airport.

We also owe just as much to the people who helped us find our brilliant gardeners, enabling us to connect with stories the world over. We would especially like to thank Aaron Deemer, Catherine Karnow, Zahid Sardar, Jared Braiterman, Osanna Avanesova, Michelle Woo, Christopher Sturman, and Lexie and Casper Mork-Ulnes.

Super-special thanks also go to the long-suffering Benjamin Doherty for letting us take over his home and garden, and fill it with plant and material supplies, and not least of all for keeping us going with a production line of culinary masterpieces. To Amy Conochie for allowing us to shoot our practical guides in her own tiny garden, to Jason Dewees, horticulturist and palm broker, for his help identifying tricky plants, and to Sheli Rodney for her skilful headline work.

Last but not least, thank you to Katie, Krissy, Laura, Hilary and the entire team at Pavilion Books for commissioning us to undertake this book, and for all of your hard work since.

CONTENTS

INTRODUCTION

'So how tiny is tiny?' people quiz, when you mention that you're working on a book about small gardens. It's a natural question to ask but a tough one to answer. You can decide, when choosing which stories to share, to make a book of gardens that accord with certain set dimensions. But for a book that spans the world? You quickly discover that those set dimensions are difficult to define.

What a Los Angeles gardener might consider woefully miniscule would, for a Londoner or New Yorker, be a veritable stately home garden, the likes of which they could only dream of. That said, tiny gardens are, in a world spun by estate agents, gaining ground. Urban homes are smaller yet more expensive than ever, and no matter what city you live in, those constraints are intensely felt. But despite all this, people are passionately embracing gardening as never before: it is taking root in every nook imaginable.

Why some decide to green up awkward spaces is because they know that gardens are about so much more than pristine topiary or palatial lawns. To garden is to speak. Small gardens can be a statement about the way you see the world beyond you. Want to rage against climate change and wildlife habitat destruction? Voice it all from a window box.

A small garden can be about simpler things, too. Ask any gardener in this book what keeps them from moving to pastures new and they'll point to the plants they've sown in the soil at their feet. To garden is to make a home.

Tiny gardens can be dazzling places that stretch the physical and mental landscape, and that begins with the billion miracles and creatures that exist in just one tablespoon of earth. Whether you're watching the effects of the process in plants growing in a handful of pots, a teeny terrace or a cramped back yard, it is enough to provide a lifetime of wonder. Tiny gardens can defy limitations of space and setting but most important of all, they can defy the limitations of the imagination.

'In the invisible places
Where the first leaves start

Green breathes growth'
'Ideogram for Green', Alice Oswald

HIGH RISE HAVENS

Sedums (opposite, left) come in many colours, sizes and textures and are easy to grow in containers.

Jared's beautiful handmade ceramic pots (opposite, right) bring personality to this small space.

Green curtains, created with a net and climbing plants, are a great way to introduce vertical space and privacy.

ORIENT EXCESS

Maximalists to the core, Jared Braiterman and Shu Kuge see no reason why the garden on their narrow balcony space in Tokyo should behave any differently to them. Plants mingle happily, like the hip guests of their renowned Saturday night parties. But their garden balcony is more than just a happy mingling of friends. Typhoons, earthquakes and oppressive summer heat – this balcony has seen them all and knows how to survive a tough urban climate.

'The tropical temperatures here mean you can grow plants that are huge and fun,' says American-born Jared. 'And no matter how busy the balcony gets, I'm always thinking I can get just one more plant in. There are shrubs, succulents, edibles, flowers – it isn't that well planned but it's pretty much everything we like.'

While traditional Japanese gardeners embrace conservative simplicity in tight spaces, Jared and partner Shu are proponents of excess. 'We're absolutely not into that minimalist aesthetic. It's such a waste in a tiny space. A garden has more impact when it's packed full. It has more stories to tell you,' says artist Shu.

Jared and Shu's south-facing apartment on the tenth floor of a 1970s housing block in western Tokyo receives generous levels of light that help to nurture their large horticultural family. Sun-loving plants such as the fig, (*Ficus carica*), are therefore highly productive, and this particular beauty is also perfectly situated in a container by a sheltering wall.

Seasonal extremes have been catered for in the space the two have lived alongside for seven years. A green curtain of twining *Ipomoea indica* diffuses the intensity of the sun's rays and provides privacy. Its striking purple-blue, funnel-shaped flowers are Jared's favourite: 'Their colour is the focal point and it blooms from late spring to autumn.' Evergreen *Olea europaea* and a camellia bequeath their colour when harsh winters render all other signs of chlorophyll pale.

Loud and lush, this garden stimulates the imagination. For Shu, the balcony, which seduces dragonflies, butterflies and the Japanese white-eye bird, is a bridge to the city: 'Urban gardens are often described as an escape but I don't really see it like that. Out here I always feel part of the city; it reinvigorates my love for Tokyo.'

White railings and white walls provide a uniform backdrop for a large variety of plant forms, and make this 5m² (54ft²) balcony feel larger.

This packed out space still feels light and airy, thanks to these wire-framed window boxes. Solid ones would make the small area feel cluttered.

The artist, whose love of plants was inspired by Jared, believes that small proportions in a garden make it more integral to a home than rolling expanses of green: 'You're always next to the garden. It's already nearby, whatever you're doing.'

Design anthropologist Jared has a different relationship with the space; it sends his mind beyond Tokyo, to the ocean. 'In our balcony garden time and stillness coexist,' he explains.

Propagation adds another dimension. Jared and Shu harvest seeds from their *Cardiospermum halicacabum*, a sub-tropical vine that produces papery seed capsules like 'green testicles' as well as from their *Ipomoea indica*, and gift them to friends. Some they keep and plant again to give the balcony continuity.

But every year there's something different to look at. 'We grow one crazy plant a year, just one. Melons, cucumbers, peas – we've had them all up here,' giggles Jared. This year it's sunflowers because 'they'll be big and crazy'.

Beyond that, there's no real plan. 'We're really lazy. It's just a question of how much we can cram into the garden. That's the aim.'

HOW TO: KOKEDAMA HANGING GARDEN

Kokedama – Japanese for 'moss ball' – are a really nifty way of utilising the space in a small garden, as they can be hung above borders, in balconies, or across passageways to provide colour and interest. They can also be adapted for indoor use as part of a houseplant display. Making kokedama for the first time can be a bit tricky, but stick with it and after a few attempts you'll get the hang of it. For outdoor kokedama, choose plants such as *Pelargonium* species that will tolerate drying out between waterings. Most hanging-basket plants will do well. It can also be fun to bring two or more plants together to produce a variety of textures and colours in one kokedama. I have used a combination of trailing and upright plants to maximise the contrast.

1. Remove the plant from its pot and shake off any excess compost.

2. If you are using more than one plant, gently tie the root balls together using twine.

3. Lay out a length of twine, ready to go, and then a piece of moss on top big enough to wrap around the ball. This makes the later tying stage much easier.

4. In a bucket, mix 2 parts multi-purpose compost with 1 part akadama – a clay-like mineral that is often used for bonsai.

5. Gradually add water and mix to create a wet (but not soggy) paste. Scoop up a large handful and gradually start shaping it into a ball.

6. As you continue shaping, the ball will become more smooth and solid.

7. Gently twist the ball apart to separate it into two rough halves.

8. With the halves in your hands, scoop up your plants' roots and start moulding them into one ball. If any gaps appear that won't close, add a pinch more mixture and continue moulding.

9. Place the ball on the moss layer and start wrapping the moss around it. Tie the twine around the middle of the moss ball to start to secure it.

10. Wrap the twine around the ball, criss-crossing as you go to hold the moss in place. Tie the twine off, leaving a length for hanging.

Your kokedama is ready to go. Here I have used an ivy-leaf geranium with *Dichondra* 'Silver Falls'.

AFTERCARE & TIPS

Kokedama need to be watered every other day in summer. The best way to do this is to soak them in a bucket of water for 5–10 minutes. Hang up to drain outside or over a dish if you are hanging your kokedama indoors. Make sure you use akadama, not bonsai compost; bonsai compost does not contain the clay particles your kokedama need.

SECATEURS IN THE CITY

Stylist Lara Backmender is sought after for her ability to create eye-catching campaigns for her A-lister editorial, advertising and celebrity clientele. But in the privacy of her Brooklyn balcony garden she combines her talent for design with a love of nature that brings her peace amid a fizzing city.

With cup of coffee in one hand, smartphone in the other, and a to-do list as long as the Brooklyn Bridge, Lara is unmistakably a New Yorker. Her restful 19m² (202ft²) balcony, however, is anything but.

'I live in a rectangular box. Everything about this building is linear and sharp,' says Lara, 'so I wanted to take this modern space and warm it up.'

Before planning her garden, Lara knew she needed to breathe air into her life, which was dense with a tough schedule of shoots, travel and emails. Designing a nurturing space was therefore the natural choice. 'I work all the time. I love the concrete urban jungle but it beats you up. I grew up in a small farm town surrounded by Mom and Dad's plants, and I still have that need to be grounded by nature,' she says, happily wielding a hose around her containers.

This chic tabletop succulent planter (above right) was a gift from Lara's sister. Native to deserts, succulents love low moisture, dry air, bright sunshine, good drainage and high temperatures.

Lara grows a small amount of herbs on her balcony, like mint and chives (right). But her plants are mostly ornamental to keep the space low-maintenance. 'Vegetable gardens are a lot of work,' she says.

Lara's love of plants comes from a childhood spent in her parents' garden. 'You put plants in a place and you feel rooted to it. A garden brings comfort and it soothes. Plants give me what I need. I feel that, technically, people can't live without them.'

Ornamental grasses (below), with their feathery and ethereal textures, bring serenity to an urban plot.

Her vision evolved by tearing pages from garden magazines, taking her time to research how best to shape the garden of her first home. She then honed her ideas on a stack of mood boards. 'In the end it came together organically. I needed to live in the space long enough to understand what I wanted from it,' she reveals.

Lara has since brought in sleepy ornamental grasses that draw the eye to a planter stretching the width of the balcony that fulfils her desire for an English meadow effect. Their calming, willowy backdrop contrasts with low-rise edging plants such as *Sutera cordata* and the violet-spiked *Veronica spicata* 'Blue Carpet' – a combination that provides the container with a huge range of visual interest.

She has softened the hard surfaces with clambering orange-flowered clematis, *Sedum* 'Blue Spruce' and *Lamium maculatum* 'Pink Pewter', while a piece of weather-beaten wood from Coney Island, now a tabletop, has the same warming effect and offers seaside charm. Nautical accessories bought from ships chandlers and seaside plants such as sea thrift (*Armeria maritima* 'Splendens') complement the look.

Lara rises early enough so she can potter before leaving the house.

'I let up my shades in the lounge and see the birds and butterflies. It's wonderful,' she explains. And when she returns at night she never walks past the garden without stopping to explore. 'I love it when new leaves have started to bud while I've been away from home. It feels like a blessing.'

Lara's controlled but naturalistic style is influenced by the Connecticut garden she grew up in, where her parents taught her so much: her mother how to raise edibles and her father, the art of maintenance. 'My dad was so proud of their garden. He would give people tours,' she remembers. 'Dad loved his garden to be precise, with no leaf out of place. That was formative for me but I wanted my own garden to be a touch less manicured.'

Over the years Lara has got to grips with the extreme New York climate, losing plants along the way. Winters are characteristically long and harsh, so to protect her pots from cracking during these snowy days, she coils sailing rope around her ceramic planters and fixes it with duct tape.

Pots on wheels under a roof at the back of the balcony mean that frost-sensitive, tender plants can be repositioned for protection and it's also a savvy solution that's perfect for moving her shade-loving species about. These planters also host ferns, such as *Adiantum pedatum*. They enjoy their shady spot under the roof, which shields a portion of the balcony, but are easily moved from undercover to catch rain when it falls. 'Ferns remind me of being a child in the stream at the bottom of my back yard. It was full of them. I love their bold shapes,' she says.

A plan to screen off the balcony space next door happily faded after her lovely neighbours moved in. 'I'm so glad I didn't go ahead with that idea. They really care for their plants, and we share that.' A trellis thick with ivy and blackberry does offer her privacy from the street, however, which is handy on those summer days when she hooks up her blue and white hammock and cocoons herself in it with a book.

The soft autumnal shades of red in the leaves of her much-cherished Acer palmatum (above) and in her succulents contrast well with the hard grey floor tiles.

Lara's treasured plants might arrive up here following weekend trips to the local nursery but are just as often gifted by her green-fingered relatives. This family trait was inspired by the Botanical Gardens just up Lara's street. 'My dad, who's from Brooklyn, was inspired to move out of the city by the Botanical Gardens so he could have his own garden. Now I live so close and that story has come full circle.

'My dad loves it when I call him and talk about my garden. My sister has a new apartment and my parents are helping to teach her about plants, too,' says Lara. 'Gardening keeps us all connected. I love it that nature has stayed with me, that it can still give me so much joy.'

The blackberry (opposite, right) could easily take over in a small space but Lara tames it with regular pruning. Blackberries work well in containers: a single plant can be highly productive and even more so given a sunny, sheltered spot.

*Several groups of containers provide
a harmonious display but each group is
made up of plants with contrasting textures,
to offer plenty of interest for the eye.*

HEAVEN IN HARLEM

Writer, gardener, forager and cook, Marie Viljoen learnt to garden before she learnt to read. So when she moved to New York City, she was never going to be deterred by its tiny apartments from creating a garden that fulfilled each one of her heart's desires.

Surrounded on all sides by high-rise housing blocks, fire escape staircases and sirens, Marie's wild Harlem rooftop terrace is a drop of heaven brimming with soul.

Tiny, sun-starved and overlooked by the neighbours, it is easy to forget all these limitations when you're up there, reclining amid the flame lilies (*Gloriosa superba*) and sipping one of Marie's cocktails, infused with berries plucked from plants growing right by your feet.

But as a lady well versed in the harsh realities of the New York renter's lot, she's becoming rather adept at cooking up a life that makes no compromises.

Vivacious Marie and her charming French husband, Vincent Mounier, moved here in 2013 from an even smaller apartment in Brooklyn, where her tiny garden experiments and love affair with the smallness of botanical life began.

That Brooklyn terrace – dubbed '66 Square Feet' (6m²) after its minute proportions – matured into a feisty plot of edibles and ornamentals. 'I was unapologetic about the space and that was important,' she says of the garden that was busy with plants and packed-out parties where copious Bellinis were served.

Her realisation that life could be lived to the max on such a microscopic terrace turned into a blog and subsequently into a recipe book that celebrated the garden's seasonal harvests. 'I'm deeply affected by the details of the seasons and that's what makes gardening important for me,' says Marie, who hunts Manhattan's wilds for produce for her cooking pot. 'Fleeting flavours and flowers are compelling; they teach you the pleasure of waiting.'

Sadly, that cherished Brooklyn apartment became a passing joy when a supersonic rent hike forced Marie and Vincent out. They feared they'd never replace it. But stepping onto this 21m² (225ft²) roof area for the first time helped them come to terms with the uprooting.

At several times the size of '66 Square Feet', the terrace gifted them a fresh and a (relatively) grand stage upon which to garden, cook and entertain. Marie and Vincent handed the landlord a cheque and signed on the dotted line.

'Sociability is important to me. I love having people over for supper and Vincent and I eat in the garden every day in good weather,' says Marie, who's been cooking since she was 14. 'Plants are a constant in my life; they connect everything I do.'

She has since filled the terrace with statuesque verticals, creating a sense of both intimacy and escape. A privacy screen made from birch trunks is a focal point and establishes a feeling of height. The snow-white bark of the birches brightens the dark space. 'Vertical plants are crucial in a small area and that's something that's so often overlooked,' says the former opera singer.

Scarlet runner beans (*Phaseolus coccineus*), scale the birch trellis, along with other plants that go up, such as lablab beans (*Lablab purpureus*). On the main deck, *Nicotiana sylvestris* and *N. mutabilis*, with its large elliptic dark green leaves, will reach up to 1.5m (60in) in their containers. They also smell wonderful at night, and are irresistible to hummingbirds.

The lush vigour of this jungle belies the fact that the garden can receive both blazing light and deep shade on the same day. 'It's been interesting dealing with that,' reveals Marie. 'Plants don't evolve to cope in those conditions – they're usually adapted to one or the other.'

Marie has cleverly introduced a birch trellis (opposite, above right) to detract attention from the buildings that surround the garden.

Black raspberries (opposite, below centre) are hugely productive on a shady terrace as Marie has discovered.

White flowers and light floral tones keep this dark space bright and cheerful.

Fascinated with what can be grown in these awkward circumstances, Marie has embraced species that are adapted to shade and has placed them in the understorey of other shrubs. Her blueberry plants (*Vaccinium corymbosum*) are therefore especially happy. Equally content are the shade-tolerant *Impatiens capensis* 'stolen from nearby woodland'. Peachy foxgloves, native to woodland edges, bloom beautifully in the changeable light.

Marie's new landscape has taught her much: that black raspberry plants are fabulous in small spaces because they perform better in shade than their red cousins. And as for the sprightly herbs that have emerged from planters on the wall: 'They were a welcome surprise,' says Marie. 'I used to think herbs needed six hours of light a day but they clearly don't.'

I quiz Marie, who has designed rooftop gardens for Manhattan's fabulously wealthy, about her 'process'. 'A process? No! I'm the worst when it comes to designing my own gardens,' she says modestly. 'My gardens are about instinct.'

This garden then, is made from and for the heart. 'Roses. I know, I know, they're old-fashioned,' she says, gesturing to the containers by the door. 'But they remind me of my childhood birthdays, which coincided with the first blooming of the roses in my mother's garden. Look at them. They're not happy but I insist on having them.' She laughs mischievously. 'And they make great cut flowers for the house.'

Wildlife doesn't discriminate between large and small gardens. This urban terrace is teeming with birds, bees and, at night, fire flies.

Tobias always dreamed of having a sunken garden. As this is not possible on a roof, he reversed the concept and has edged the garden with planters instead.

Engineers tested the rooftop's suitability for the 5,000 litres (177 cubic feet) of earth and hefty containers they'd envisaged. Heavy items positioned close to the edge of the roof spread the weight.

ROOFTOP RETREAT

Tobias Mandelartz and Dirk Bernecker's atmospheric rooftop cottage garden in a leafy suburb of Berlin is a stage set of rooms, each with its own personality.

This rooftop may not be large, but it's the largest garden Tobias and Dirk have ever lived with, so they let themselves dream.

When they sat down to plan their 80m² (860ft²) of space, they knew they wanted the effect of both wilderness and formality – contrasting styles that are not easy to master in a small space.

But they summoned the spirit of German nurseryman Karl Foerster for inspiration, and his talent for dividing gardens into separate rooms each with a distinct purpose is honoured here.

Cottage plants like rose and *Allium giganteum* have been beautifully arranged around the sun deck. Just in the 'next door room', neat domes of *Buxus sempervirens* pose on a lawn as a nod to English formality. Terracotta pots exude Mediterranean chic and Tobias and Dirk have planted a herb garden along a wall. 'We're proud of it, like it was our child,' Tobias beams.

Again emulating Foerster, Tobias has chosen plants not because of their particular colour or to fulfil a specific concept. 'Foerster saw a plant as an individual with its own reason for being,' Tobias says of his horticultural hero.

'Trees offer privacy and escape,' says Tobias.

Edging the roof is a collection of trees thriving in pots, such as silver birch, photinia and *Acer platanoides*. 'We wanted trees. Every home needs them,' says Tobias, an online journalist, who spends most of his day out here, pottering, preparing food or reclining in his deckchair.

This dream was realised in just nine weeks, and Tobias and Dirk are now revelling in their flushes of floral success, as well as enjoying the butterflies and nesting blue tits besides. 'We're never moving,' says Tobias. 'A garden roots you to a place, much more than a house.'

HOW TO:
NIGHT-SCENTED POTS

Feel the benefit of your outdoor space in the evening, when night-scented plants release their fragrance to attract moths and other nocturnal insects. A cluster of night-scented pots carefully positioned by an open back door or window will fill the air with truly delicious perfumes. If you are lucky enough to have a seating area in your garden, place your pots nearby so you can relax and enjoy the evening scent after a hard day's work. You can use any container for your scented plants, just as long as it has drainage holes. More important is the choice of plants. Here I have used the tobacco plants, *Nicotiana affinis,* and *N. alata* 'Grandiflora', and the evening primrose cultivar, *Oenothera speciosa* 'Twilight'.

1. Line the bottom of your pot with coarse gravel or crocks – broken pieces of terracotta – to stop soil clogging up the drainage hole.

2. Remove your plant from its pot, remove any dead or damaged foliage and place the plant in its container. Use a good quality loam-based compost to fill in around the root ball.

3. Add extra impact to the planting with some bedding plants around the edge. These petunias are sweetly scented, too.

A honey bee happily feeding on an evening primrose flower.

AFTERCARE & TIPS

Keep your pots well watered during summer, making sure the compost does not dry out as this will stress the plants.

Other plants to try: Night-scented stock (*Matthiola longipetala* subsp. *bicornis*), *Phlox paniculata* 'Eventide', night-scented phlox (*Zaluzianskya ovata*)

HARMONY AND HUE

**London's Barbican is a post-war housing and arts complex, built in the Brutalist architectural style.
It is covered in a concrete façade and situated amid the sky-rise towers of the city's financial markets.
This is where William Howard has lived for over two decades. And where, one window box at
a time, he's conjured a narrow balcony into an award-winning garden that sings.**

William's garden possesses what pop culture might describe as 'The X Factor'. Standing by the
lake at the centre of the complex, it is clear that many a Barbican resident takes pride in their
balcony space.

But this one is a leading lady amid a chorus.

Plants spill, in Rapunzel cascades, over the austere balcony front. Plant spill from above, too. And
window boxes dazzle with floral yellows, pinks, reds and purples.

The former civil engineer – who spent much time during his career with concrete – clearly knows
how to bring out the best in it.

Known as the 'Hanging Gardens of Barbican', this balcony has attracted armfuls of accolades.
And although William is too modest to admit it, his efforts and his role as Chair of the Barbican
Horticultural Society over 12 years, have inspired countless neighbours to conjure their own
austere balconies into splendour.

But this public performance is only one side of the story. William, with big sweeps of his arm,
waves us up to join him in the living room of 108 Gilbert House for an insight into the private soul
of this 15m^2 (160ft^2) of space.

'To me this is two different gardens. The public one softens the concrete façades. But there is a private side too,' says William.

Silvery foliage such as Artemisia 'Silver Grey' and Euphorbia characias 'Silver Swan' (below right) deepens floral colour.

Alongside shelves lined with natural history books, classical CDs and walls of family photographs, William's floor-to-ceiling composition is on display in its entire glory.

Cobaea scandens slinks across the top of the balcony. Pink begonias and hydrangeas punch the eye with staccato rhythm. And fuchsias whisper into the air from their hanging baskets. Red flowers fade and wash into pink.

William, who swapped sheep and fields in Kent for an apartment here, took his inspiration from studying Renaissance painters like Titian. 'Look at how beautiful their church paintings were. They were wonderful. They knew how to make colour speak, not like the harsh Lutherans,' says William, an irresistible bundle of energy who counts Gregorian chant and Shakespeare among his other interests. 'I've tried to offer height, depth and colour, and knit them together to give that same feeling that those artists did.'

William and his beloved partner Jenny dine out here, surrounded by trinkets from grandchildren, nesting wrens and the remembrances of years. Adventures in Andorra over four decades ago are captured in the bark of a now mature pine shrub, grown from a seed William harvested there from a cone.

Translucent model butterflies staked in window boxes represent family trips to the British Museum, where, as a ten-year old boy, William saw the tomb paintings of the Egyptian Nebamun adorned with tiger butterflies. 'Those times have stayed with me ever since,' says William, who describes himself as a 'classic Catholic cockney' born not far from where he now lives.

Memories, lovely memories,' he says, as we potter about the plants, a light wind blowing from across the lake and rustling the leaves around us. Then he turns to me with twinkling eyes, and says: 'Sometimes you see things in life and they really grab your heart, don't they?'

Indeed, they do.

SIZE ZERO HEROES

Elegant draping leaves, like this Philodendron scandens, *combined with linear leaves, create a rhythm to this garden that offsets the symmetrically arranged planters.*

WONDER WALL

At a former carpet dyeing factory in Los Angeles' Silver Lake neighbourhood, friends Deborah Burch and Faith Blakeney have created a fresh-feeling work space with a stylish, impactful indoor balcony garden.

When Deborah expanded the operation of her hip production company, Snog Productions, into this 1920s building, she wanted a space that would feel like home and would bring harmony to her hectic days.

This magical indoor greenhouse is the result. Downstairs *Philodendron scandens* and *Chlorophytum comosum* tumble and cascade overhead. Upstairs swords of *Sansevieria trifasciata* 'Laurentii', and *Monstera deliciosa*, offer a calm living room space so captivating that it is easy to forget the computer in the corner.

When Deborah moved in she was looking to dress the industrial concrete space with succulents but soon realised that their need for high levels of light could not be met in that space. Then friend Faith, an interior designer, got involved and the pair drew up plans for a jungle garden that would thrive in this indoor setting.

Claiming floor area wasn't an option: the studio needs floor space to function properly at times when Snog Productions takes on more staff and props during busy periods.

A living wall, therefore, felt like the perfect solution. 'We had to build a structural wall first,' says Deborah. 'This hides the irrigation system, which supplies water on a drip-feed system through copper pipes connected to the bathroom plumbing. Concealing these mechanics inside the wall gives the plants a floating effect.'

A vibrant living balcony provides this busy work environment with fresh air and calms the atmosphere. 'I interact with a lot of people during the day, taking care of their needs. So it's nice to get away from the computer and check in with my plants. It puts your head in a different space,' says Deborah.

Faith's final composition, of around 100 plants, is arranged in three rows of planters. 'I selected plants based on a lot of research about which would be happiest in the loft,' she remembers. 'Once at the garden centre I set them out on the ground outside and played with different arrangements, according to the measurements of the 15m x 3m (49ft x 11ft) wall.'

Enlisting slow-growing species was crucial for keeping the original composition intact and in proportion. As one of the signature plants, the tropical sansevieria's dawdling growth helps maintain a visual balance between the upper and lower levels of the garden. While in the lower reaches of the garden, the plants are allowed to hang free. Common to all the plant choices, however, was that they must have similar light, water and air requirements.

Maintaining a wall on this scale takes work. In addition to daily TLC from Deborah, ensuring the irrigation is working well means regular visits from the installers. Early disasters, before the system calibration was perfected, included a weekly three-minute rain shower from the wall. 'It took a while to get right. And we had to watch the plants to see how they got on. Time is important in making a garden like this thrive,' advises Faith.

A space like Deborah's may not be within the reach of many, but the girls encourage anyone to try their own indoor wall garden at home. The important factors are easy access to a water supply, even if it is DIY, and providing the correct light conditions for your plant choices.

Although Snog Productions' workspace is only rented, Deborah believes the investment has definitely been worth it: 'The garden helps me escape from my work. I can step away from my desk to do some watering and it feels like I'm in another place entirely.'

Deborah's home-made terrarium is fun and contrasts with the loft's industrial feel. Here she's used air plants (Tillandsia), which can root themselves in a variety of places. Learn how to create your own on terrarium on page 58.

Living wall planters, as here, can be used to create a modular garden as big or as tiny as the space allows. Opt for species that will spill over the edges, such as Philodendron scandens, and those that will fill in empty spaces, such as dieffenbachia.

Creating a style that reflected a California vibe was key for Deborah (left) and interior designer Faith (right) – resulting in a garden that feels fun, wild and free.

HOW TO: DESKTOP GARDEN

Enliven your workspace with a size zero cactus and succulent planter. Using small-scale plants allows you to create a fascinating range of textures and colours in a tiny space. I have chosen two miniature wooden chests as my ideal portable containers. The drawers can be swapped around to make new arrangements. Desert cacti and succulents are perfect plants for small and unusual containers, since they need very little soil and mostly favour dry conditions. They are best positioned next to a sunny window, as they like to receive at least four hours' direct sunlight to thrive, and sometimes flower. Turn your desktop garden periodically so the plants receive light from all sides. If you do not have a sunny spot, use jungle cacti instead. They have similar requirements but do not like direct sunlight.

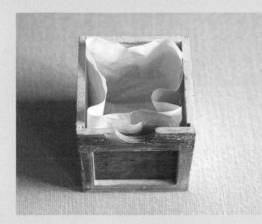

1. Line the box with a piece of plastic to protect the wood – an old plastic shopping bag works fine.

2. Add a layer of coarse gravel to the bottom of the box for drainage.

Everyone loves the 'Bunny Ears' cactus and the little pink flowers of the mimicry plant (*Frithia pulchra*), otherwise known as fairy elephant's feet.

AFTERCARE & TIPS

Water your plants regularly during spring and summer, letting the compost almost dry out between waterings. Always use specialised cacti and succulent compost as it has a high sand content that suits these plants. Check out your local aquatic centre for the fine gravel you need as a topping; they often carry a greater range than garden centres.

3. Add the cacti, one at a time and gently fill in with compost using a teaspoon. Don't firm the compost too much, and make sure it does not come too high up the cactus.

4. Add a layer of fine gravel around the plants, covering all the compost. The plants I am using here are the 'Bunny Ears' cactus (*Opuntia microdasys*) and *Pleiospilos nelii* 'Rubra'.

Desert cacti to try: *Mammillaria elongata, Opuntia subulata, Pilosocereus glaucochrous*
Succulents to try: *Aloe peglerae, Pachyphytum oviferum, Sedum* 'Burrito'

FLOATING FLORA

Matt Wright, landscaper and designer, and his partner, Izabella Doyle, live on *Chinampa*, a barge in London, with their cat Peter.

They may not have known a huge amount about boats when they made the leap from land to water, but what they were sure of was that their new home had to be as much of a sanctuary for their collection of plants as for themselves.

When Matt and Izabella made their first home together, it was the plants that came first. 'Boats can be dark and pokey but we wanted a space that brought light in for our plants,' says Matt. 'So when we designed our boat we did it by thinking through where the windows would be, and therefore where the plants would sit. And we also planned where best to place the stove that would help keep our tropical plants alive.'

Their floating garden is a triumph. *Chinampa* is cleverly designed with a large light well that spans the corridor between the bedroom and living area, and that washes their indoor plants with photosynthetic goodness. And an outdoor garden at the stern hosts a lovingly curated collection of plants and an ever-changing selection of specimens destined for Matt's clients' gardens.

Matt and Izabella's garden provides sanctuary in London's urban landscape. 'Sometimes we moor in places where there's no green at all and those can be harsh environments for us. Our garden is both our balance and our escape,' says Izabella.

Possessing an exquisite eye for interior design, Matt, a trained fine artist, and Izabella, a freelance pattern cutter, have made plants the visual focal point of their barge home. The muted tones in their white walls and grey floors combine with mid-century furnishings to make the fleshy greens of their indoor garden wholly arresting.

'Whenever we look at people's homes in magazines, the ones we're always drawn to are the ones that have lots of plants,' says Izabella. 'It doesn't matter what type of building or what the style is, plants change the atmosphere of a place completely.'

With so much attention focused on them, it is little wonder that their plants look so happy. Fleshy succulents spring from hanging baskets, and there are pots full of ficus, *Monstera deliciosa*, and numerous cacti, both large and small.

What is notable though, is how comfortable the garden seems in this ever-changing climate. Matt and Izabella do not have permanent moorings in the city, which means that they must move their house at least every two weeks. And the boat's extreme temperatures, which plummet as summer's heat turns to winter's damp, have been tough on plants that mostly herald from hot, dry climates.

'It's a tricky environment for the plants as conditions change so much through the year. The first winter we didn't have a stove and it was really tough. Our big banana plant didn't survive. But now the stove keeps the boat at a constant temperature,' says Matt.

The couple also ensure that as they move from one mooring to the next, they keep light conditions constant. 'We try not to park under trees and are aware where the sun is coming from in any new mooring, and at what point in the day it hits the boat,' Izabella explains.

Out on the stern there is an entirely new set of conditions to consider. Exposure to wind means the garden can dry out quickly and needs daily watering.

Here they have focused on seasonal interest, with a young *Pseudopanax lessonii*, which can withstand frosts and can grow up to 6m (20ft) and a *Muehlenbeckia complexa*, which loves to climb. Both are evergreen and provide colour and structure at the stern through colder months. A *Dodonaea viscosa* offers pleasing dark red foliage during the autumn. All hail from New Zealand.

The position of every succulent, cacti and trailing plant has been carefully considered to avoid cluttering up this tiny houseboat.

Matt and Izabella focus on varying the tones of green in foliage rather than focusing on flowers because flowers are short-lived. 'In a small garden you need to think about the structural element to ensure you have something interesting all through the year,' says Matt.

'You often find these plants living by the coast in poor sandy conditions and high winds so they are well suited to boat life,' explains Matt. But there's stuff you might not have expected to thrive here too; an *Echeveria elegans*, native to Mexico, is boasting a flush of spikes tipped with little lantern-shaped pink flowers.

The constantly changing landscapes in their life inspire Matt and Izabella in their plant choices outside. Noticing prolific amounts of buddleja as they roam alongside the banks of London's waterways prompted them to bring a dwarf version of this butterfly magnet on board.

Grasses, inspired by their trips to Hackney Marshes along the River Lea, are here for the same reason. 'There are so many native grasses around the marshes, so it's good to have them here. I like to contextualise what I do here with my surroundings.'

Matt, who's learnt the horticultural trade by working rather than studying, says that feeling that there are garden design 'rights and wrongs' can be restrictive and can deter creativity, especially in awkward spaces.

'I haven't tied myself to any rules,' says Matt. 'I don't know what's officially correct but I see that as a huge benefit. I work with my senses and that gives me freedom.'

HOW TO: INDOOR WINDOW GARDEN

Even if you have no outside space at all you can still bring a range of greenery into your living space by creating a garden in your window. With a little DIY and some careful arranging, you can produce a beautiful foliage display to enjoy all year round. This can be particularly useful in an office situation, or if you work from home, as it is widely proven that growing plants in the workspace reduces stress, increases oxygen levels and aids productivity. You can make a window garden in any window, large or small, whether it is north or south-facing, but you must make sure it is not directly above a radiator as the heat will damage the plants in winter. My window garden is mainly north-facing, but it receives about two hours of strong evening sunlight in summer.

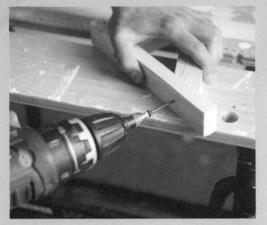

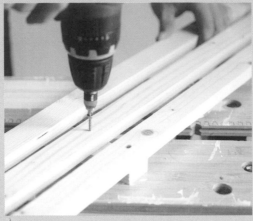

1. Start by assembling two triangular brackets using wooden battens from any DIY store. Allow enough wood on the back of the bracket to attach it to the window frame (see Step 5). Alternatively you can buy ready-made brackets and customise them.

2. Make a simple slatted shelf to the width you require, with a short batten in the middle for stability.

3. Paint your shelf any colour you like using interior wood paint. This will protect the wood from general wear and tear.

4. Once dry, offer the shelf up to the window frame and check with a spirit level before marking the position of the shelf with a pencil.

5. Screw the bracket into the window frame.

6. Start arranging your plants, putting the trailing plants at the top so they can grow downwards. Keep more delicate foliage plants at the front where they can be appreciated.

Have some fun decorating the spaces between your plants with little sculptures and other items of interest.

Here I am hanging a small piece of handmade stained glass from a hook attached to the underside of the shelf to catch the light behind the foliage.

AFTERCARE & TIPS

Keep your houseplants well watered during the growing season. As a general rule of thumb, allow the top of the compost to dry out between waterings. Most houseplants will grow in a range of indoor situations but some have more specific requirements about how much direct sunlight they need. Always consult a good reference book to make sure.

Plants to try in a sunny window: rubber plant (*Ficus elastica*), *Aloe vera*, *Sansevieria trifasciata* 'Laurentii'
Plants to try in a shady window: *Dracaena sanderiana*, *Maranta leuconeura*, *Nephrolepis exaltata*

BORDER BEATS

New Yorker Alejandro Aguilar is a master of small-space solutions after years spent living in minuscule apartments turned him to a career redesigning little homes. With a pointillist's eye for design, he explores every tiny bit of space to inject interiors and gardens with style, discipline and personality.

'This is just the beginning,' says Alejandro, with a magician's sweep to draw back a heavy curtain.

As he opens the door behind, we step into a sun-blushed yard, bursting with colour, composition and scent.

Alejandro arrived here only a few weeks ago at the LP 'N Harmony Bar in Williamsburg, Brooklyn, answering an SOS call from its owners who were desperate for help with their barren 81m² (870ft²) yard.

Jede Brahma and John Clemente were seeking a haven for jasmine, roses and honeysuckle, and a place to grow mint for their mojito cocktails. But they were at a loss over how to introduce such a garden to a yard that also needed to be used for dancing.

But when it comes to small-space challenges, there's none too big – or small – for Alejandro. 'I'm no gardener,' he admits, 'but I have a no-nonsense approach. I tell my clients that the first step to helping themselves is to admit that they live in a tiny place and to deal with it.'

The garden is still a work in progress but Alejandro has already conjured up a savvy solution for Jede – a moveable mint garden consisting of large but portable planters handmade from wood salvaged from a dumpster.

Comprising several separate containers that slot together like pieces of a jigsaw, Alejandro has turned it mobile with castors fixed underneath. This allows Jede and John to shift the planters to one side or separate them on busy nights.

Bright borders decked with colour now surround three sides of the yard. From far away, bold leaves define the borders, but as you move closer, different focal points come into view. This means that each plant can compete for attention in its own unique way. Bold-leaved plants such as hydrangeas have therefore been arranged alongside the medium-sized foliage of *Hosta* 'Shade Fanfare' and the small-leaved foliage of *Lychnis coronaria*.

'Textural design' says Alejandro, who also teaches classes on tiny spaces, 'must be your starting point before you fill your garden-centre trolley. I love leaves more than flowers. They give depth and a layered effect.'

He works with one section of border at a time to create small compositions of plants, giving the viewer multiple 'paintings' to look at. 'I find people often don't think about a sense of position,' says Alejandro. 'Examine each section of the space in turn,' he adds. 'And remember your eye will be drawn to a focal point first and then wander towards everything else.'

'I like to create a series of little gardens within one space, even one border. The more you can plant within a frame the better,' says Alejandro.

Incorporating scent was an important element for Jede, one of the bar's co-owners, so they have introduced lavender, mint, thyme and honeysuckle to the borders. 'I'm out here every day now,' she says. 'It's such a peaceful space.'

HOW TO: AQUATIC TERRARIUM

Create a micro garden with a difference using aquatic and marginal plants in an unusual glass container of your choice. Marginal plants will grow and produce leaves above and below the water's surface. I've used a glass vivarium I found in a pet shop, but you could use any transparent watertight container, or re-purpose an old fish tank. An aquatic terrarium is a perfect solution if you don't have space for lots of containers, and it can fit easily on a desk, bookshelf or windowsill. Although terrariums are intricate to assemble, they are very low-maintenance – you'll just need to top up the water when it starts to get low.

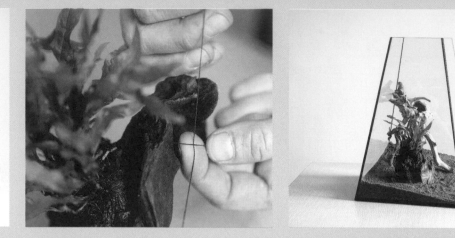

1. Fill the bottom of the terrarium with aquatic substrate to provide a root zone for the plants. Creating a slope makes it look more dynamic.

2. Plants such as the Java fern (*Microsorum pteropus*) attach themselves to wood in the wild. Use dark cotton thread to tie the plant to a piece of pre-soaked ornamental bogwood for a natural look.

3. Arrange the bogwood along with other pieces of wood, stone or roots in the terrarium.

4. Add a 2cm (¾in) layer of fine aquatic gravel to completely cover the substrate. Choose a colour similar to the substrate as this looks more natural.

5. Add more plants by gently pushing them into the substrate so that their roots are covered. Try and keep taller plants at the back.

6. Slowly start to fill the terrarium with water, pouring it onto the wood to stop the gravel from being disturbed.

7. Fill the terrarium about one-third full so there is a good amount of foliage emerging from the water.

AFTERCARE & TIPS

Before filling your terrarium, put it in the bath and fill it with water first to be sure there are no leaks. If you are going to keep it in a dark corner of the house, attach a clip-on LED aquarium lamp to the top to make sure the plants have enough light. You can get all your supplies from a good aquatic centre, where you can also get advice on which plants to choose.

Plants to try: *Alternanthera reineckii, Anubias gilletii, Cryptocoryne beckettii*

Enjoy how the underwater landscape contrasts with the emerging foliage.

BIJOU BACK YARDS

SEASIDE ROMANCE

When Christopher Stocks and partner Roy Barker moved into their eighteenth-century seaside cottage in Dorset's Isle of Portland, they arrived with bags of ideas for its small and neglected back garden.

Within a year, they'd turned a boring yard with a shed and an awkward-looking camellia into a romantic, riotous space full of life and colour.

Chris and Roy bring complementary skills to their 24m² (258ft²) spot. Chris, an editor and writer, is the design guru, while Roy, a customer database director and self-confessed 'data geek', is the plantsman whose forensic knowledge is the guiding force across every scrap of soil.

This garden proves that tiny spaces can be playgrounds for passionate horticulturalists. 'Roy can't stop planting. He loves plants and wants as many here as possible,' says Chris, affectionately. 'Our problem is trying to find any one plant among all the rest!'

They are therefore advocates for diminutive garden plots. 'By the first summer the garden more or less looked like it does now,' says Roy. 'People think a tiny space is a drawback but it requires less maintenance, and you can transform it quickly.'

Chris and Roy don't place too many functional demands on this garden, leaving as much room as possible for their huge collection of plants to thrive.

'I love digging, getting my hands dirty and turning compost. It's so far removed from my normal job, where I'm just looking at a computer screen. Gardening is like being a child again. And it keeps you grounded,' says Chris (left).

A maximalist approach to plants has been smartly balanced with a sensible attitude to function. The space is not overloaded with responsibility; a pathway, somewhere for a washing line and a bench to watch the sun set, are all the demands that are placed on it.

'We have no kids or pets so all we need to do is get from one end of the garden to the other. Lawns are a waste of space,' says Chris, who used to write a weekly gardening column for *The Independent*, and is a freelance editor for titles such as *House & Garden* and *Wallpaper*.

With so much room for plants, the south-west facing garden is a feast for the eyes. At ground level, hellebores vie with fritillaries. Grabbing attention higher up are floaty spears of *Chamaenerion angustifolium* 'Album' and *Nicotiana mutabilis*, whose flowers open white and gradually turn deep pink with age. There's even a corner for a bench to house Roy's impressive collective of alpines, which he nurtures from seed.

Fifteen years ago the garden consisted of a yard, some 'ratty-looking grass', a large shed and very few plants. But Chris and Roy were raring to get stuck in: their previous homes had only provided enough space to tinker with window pots, pots on steps or window boxes.

Most exciting about their new place was the fact that it had the conditions needed for a thriving garden, including generous amounts of light. 'The light is dazzling here and for a lot of the time,' says Roy. 'The reflection from the sea makes a big difference and since there's no land on the horizon, we get every last second of daylight that's on offer.' Roy's *Trachelospermum jasminoides* was especially grateful in its new home: 'It had been in three different gardens in the same pot but when it came here it behaved like it had been set free from prison,' jokes Roy.

Frosts are almost unheard of, allowing the couple to grow tender plants such as echiums, while the clay-rich soil provides a fertile, moisture-retentive medium with which to work. Use of extensive groundcover plants, like hardy geraniums, also prevents soil from drying out. 'Growing densely like this keeps the weeds away; there's no room for them to get established,' says Chris.

Being surrounded by buildings and a wall helps take the edge off the storms that can whip around the seaside village. 'Wind tends to get funnelled over the top of us. A friend of ours who lives just along the street gets the full brunt of the weather but we're lucky.' With a plant scheme that is dominated by herbaceous perennials, much of the garden is tucked underground when the worst of the Jurassic Coast weather strikes.

This being Chris and Roy's second home, the plants need to look after themselves in their absence. But since the garden has such good 'environmental genes', it helps them maintain – and enjoy – it, saying that it requires just four hours of their time a month. 'We only need to water every fortnight and that's mainly the plants in pots. What's here just has to get on with it,' says Chris. 'That's a big consideration for us because we aren't here to watch what's happening every day.'

Chris says their approach to colour and texture is 'reactive' and has been mastered simply by observing the way the garden looks throughout the year. To balance a swathe of strappy-leaved *Nerine bowdenii* and amaryllis therefore, Roy planted the *Aquilegia chrysantha*, which has larger, bolder foliage – as well as beautiful buttery flowers. 'A combination of leaf texture and colour is crucial. We plant with shades of different greens and with shapes and sizes in mind,' says Chris.

Although there's little room to do anything new just now, nature keeps things interesting for the owners of this densely packed plot: 'One great thing is that plants die every so often and that leaves space for you to do something different,' says Roy. 'There's constant change but that's what makes a garden exciting.'

With so much abundance, smaller plants can get smothered, so Roy keeps meeker specimens in pots. He advises that when choosing plants that will spread, do so with caution: 'Spreaders can be controllable or thugs. We had a white Japanese anemone that couldn't be controlled so we had to dig it out. The Chamaenerion angustifolium *'Album' is better behaved.'*

HOW TO: ALPINE WALL PLANTER

A wall planter is a great way to make the most of the wall space in a small plot. Alpine plants are a superb choice for shallow planters that cannot hold a lot of compost and moisture since alpines are adapted to grow in thin, stony soil on sunny, windswept mountainsides. Alpines are also often slow-growing and compact, making them well suited to tiny spaces. Hanging your planter at eye level will showcase the often astonishingly intricate detail of the foliage and flowers of these plants. The striking range of colours and textures they provide cannot fail to rejuvenate an unloved garden wall. Make sure you can provide good drainage as alpines do not like to sit in wet soil. Here I have used salvaged steel C-section beams as they have an attractive rustic quality, but for a more lightweight alternative you could use plastic guttering.

1. Using a metal drill bit, make a series of holes along the beam for attaching to the wall.

2. Offer the beam up to the wall to check it is level, and with a pencil, mark the holes for drilling.

3. Using a masonry drill bit, drill the marked holes. Insert good-quality wall plugs into the holes and tap them flush to the bricks with a hammer.

4. Fix the beams in place using good-quality coach screws or similar, and tighten them up with a spanner.

5. Use a strong 2-part adhesive to glue a strip of metal to the outside edges of the beam.

6. Hold the metal strip in place until the glue starts to set. These strips will hold the stones and soil in place while allowing free drainage.

7. Prop a few large pebbles against the inside edges of the metal strips to prevent the soil falling out.

8. Pour a layer of gravel in the bottom of the beam to provide good drainage.

9. Remove the plant from its pot and take off any dead or damaged leaves before planting.

Plants below include: *Dianthus* 'Little Jock', *Thymus* 'Archer's Gold', *Sisyrinchium* 'E.K. Balls', *Thymus* 'Purple Beauty' and *Sempervivum* 'Lively Bug'

10. Using a soil-based compost mixed with horticultural grit, firm in around the roots. Use a spoon to make this easier in between the plants.

11. Add a top layer of horticultural grit around the plants, taking care not to cover any leaves. This will improve drainage and prevent plants rotting at the base.

AFTERCARE & TIPS

The best time to plant alpines is in spring when the plants will have a chance to settle during the cool, moist weather. Once established, alpines are very drought-tolerant, but if you are planting in summer you will need to water well in hot, dry spells until the plants are established.

Other alpines to try: *Drosanthemum hispidum*, *Saxifraga* 'Southside Seedling', *Sedum* 'Golden Queen', *Sempervivum* 'Sprite'

TROPICAL TREASURE

Inspired by her love of Bali's temple ruins, Jo Heffernan and friends transformed the back yard of her San Francisco home from a small, sloping concrete patio into a tropical paradise. They cleverly considered every corner of space, adding dividing walls to provide separate garden 'rooms' for their vast collection of succulents, orchids, ferns and passion vines. The result is a spiritual sanctuary for all who visit.

It all began when a 1.2m (4ft) high leaping frog stole Jo's heart.

'I fell in love with this sculpture during a trip to Bali in the late eighties. It came home with me and sat on our concrete patio, grieving and surrounded by rampant raspberry plants,' she jokes. 'It kept telling me it needed the jungle.'

Much to his relief, the frog's wishes were granted.

The bones of her new garden were formed by a series of temple ruins', created by Danish engineer, Anders Dam, famed for his talent for creating unusual hardscapes.

'I like getting my hands in the dirt but I also wanted a place to think, read and be quiet,' reveals Jo.

'I've always had a need for a garden. My mother had a traditional garden full of roses. This one is different,' says Jo.

Laurentia fluviatilis (opposite, above right) is a mat-forming evergreen perennial. Jo has used it as groundcover, which gives interest at floor level and a lawn effect in this small space.

'I wanted the garden to be a sanctuary. And it is. Coming out here every morning is part of my routine. I feel so blessed to have this in my life.'

It took a year to perfect the Balinese-style walls, pillars and arches – adorned with artefacts from her Indonesian travels. Then Jo teamed up with another Dane, Sten Hojme. Together they created her jungle garden, weaving it into a tropical tapestry. The result is a graceful balance of horticultural variety that keeps the eye travelling for what feels like forever around this 44m^2 (480ft^2).

A low-growing succulent garden shimmering with pink, purple, red, gold and silver plants characterises one section, while a green wall erected to hide a large, oppressive retaining wall is thick with *Adiantum*, *Tillandsia*, *Chlorophytum comosum*, *Ficus pumila*, and *Soleirolia soleirolii*. A trickling sound from a small pond by the doorway nurtures a sense of peacefulness.

Long arching stems of clambering plants such as an exotic passion flower and *Leycesteria formosa*, which scramble over a set of original temple doors, add rhythm and textural interest. An impressive *Philodendron monstera*, native to humid tropical forests, was enlisted for its rainforest vibe. And the fragrant creamy yellow-orange flowers of the *Michelia champaca*, found in the forests of Indonesia, are a delight for hummingbirds.

All these tropical plants survive here thanks to some serendipitous climatic conditions. Sten, Jo's partner in the garden, explains: 'The garden faces due east and thanks to the stone of the patio and the walls, the garden absorbs the warmth of the morning sun and is protected from west winds by the house. It can be bitterly cold at the front but warm here, with no sound of wind at all.'

Over the years Jo and Sten have learnt that keeping a sense of scale in a small space is crucial, so they have had to remove plants that grew to dominate and drain attention from the delicate intricacies at work. A beautiful *Trachycarpus fortunei* grew from 1.5m (5ft) to 8m (25ft) – too beastly big for this tiny jungle. 'It just had to go to keep the harmony. We had a little ceremony to say farewell.'

A few carefully edited decorative pieces provide visual interest and personality, as here on this patio (opposite, below left).

A mass of clivias (opposite, right), whose striking, trumpet-shaped orange flowers provide a bright shock of colour, enlivens a dark corner. Native to the woodlands of South Africa, these plants are well suited to the lack of direct sun.

Small spaces can still include water features like this one (right). They bring a sense of calm and magic.

This garden's island forest vibe has been created with palms like Howea forsteriana *(above). They are low maintenance and shade tolerant and can be grown in containers.*

ISLE OF SUN

Sharing his home with an English wife and a Moluccan cockatoo, Kai Bansner has a small back garden in San Francisco's Mission District that is a delightful concoction of classic and tropical planting.

On the fence in Kai's back yard, hidden under a thick drape of foliage, hangs a plaque given to him by his father.

On it is inscribed what is surely one of life's universal truths, courtesy of singer–songwriter Joni Mitchell: 'We are star dust, we are golden, we are billion-year-old carbon ... and we've got to get ourselves back to the garden.'

Few would understand the sentiment better than Kai's gregarious salmon-crested cockatoo, Pooh Baer. This talkative bird from Indonesia's island of Seram, is comfortably at home in this mini forest habitat. Ferns, palms and the twinkling trickles of water falling in the pond define this 42m² (452ft²) space.

'I love spending time out here as I can spend time with Pooh. He can't enjoy himself as much sitting indoors,' says Kai, a software developer. Out in this garden Pooh takes time to relax by sunning his feathers in Kai's lemon tree, stalking the dirt or flipping over leaves on the hunt for bugs.

The garden's clay soil, which becomes dry and cracked in hotter months, means Kai has drafted in drought-tolerant yet tropical-looking plants such as a fuzzy, apple-green ornamental asparagus, *Asparagus densiflorus* 'Myers' and a *Parajubaea cocoides*, a semi drought-tolerant palm from Ecuador.

Also featuring in this tiny forest is a Colombian *Ceroxylon alpinum* and the miniature tree fern, *Blechnum gibbum*, which can grow to 1.5m (5ft) tall.

But it's not just about Pooh. Wife Natasha's wish for an English lawn has been cleverly granted in the form of Scotch moss (*Sagina subulata* 'Aurea'). This perfect small-space solution forms a carpet of bright neon-yellow, evoking a lawn-like texture. 'It needs one or two hours of light a day and a lot of water,' Kai advises.

Kai admits that he is relaxed about the design of the space, with much of what has ended up here by chance: 'It's mainly plants I've been given'.

An apple tree from his mother, the progeny of a pregnant onion plant that he bought at elementary school, roses for Natasha, and a black mission fig tree given by a friend, all dwell in this miniature forest, and it still offers room aplenty for a particularly characterful, lively bird.

COMPACT CO-OPS

'There could be more of these temporary gardens in London. The city's always being churned up and as projects can take a while to get planning permission, it's worth doing something on-site, even if it is just short-lived,' says Paul (opposite), who advises that a minimum of two years is needed to make a community garden.

Shahina and Rosemary are members of the Grow Elephant site. Shahina (right) is an artist who's joined to help paint the fences surrounding the site. 'I'm interested in seeing how the garden evolves. I like plants but haven't been able to do much with my little patch at home,' says Shahina.

URBAN MAKEOVER

Mobile Gardeners is a network of community gardeners and growing spaces. It started life as a campaign to bring more green space to Elephant and Castle in south-east London, a district undergoing huge redevelopment and otherwise known for its concrete and cars.

Led by local residents Richard Reynolds, Paul McGann and Chris Mead, the project is turning the area into a model of what can be done in small and temporary spaces, proving that the only obstacle in the way of gardens in cities is a lack of imagination.

Grow Elephant, Mobile Gardeners' newest community garden, is gradually taking shape behind construction hoardings on the New Kent Road.

One day it will be turned over for expensive flats but today it is a haven of gardening creativity, where locals without any garden or outdoor space of their own can exercise their green fingers.

It may be a new site but they are already nurturing *Tropaeolum majus* and *Calendula officinalis* in blue plastic crates and *Helichrysum italicum* among the springs of an old leather sofa. They also have plans to turn an empty bathtub into a water-lily garden.

These are not allotment spaces where the goal is to grow as much produce as possible. The aim is simply to address the effect of the demolition of the Heygate Estate. The 1970s housing block, cleared to make way for redevelopment, nursed precious green spaces that were rare in the neighbourhood.

'We saw all the green being removed and we wanted to get it back,' says Paul. 'Life can be difficult in a crowded city as people are living on top of one another. These gardens aren't big in scale but hopefully we create an interesting environment for people to take refuge in.'

Most members at the garden will grow plants in the old council recycling crates (all that's needed are a few drainage holes drilled in the bottom). 'We use containers that don't dry out too quickly. In a community space people don't tend to be here every day so we need containers that can retain water,' explains Paul, who trained as a landscape gardener.

The beauty of these containers is that it allows as many people as possible to use the site, which is freely accessible in exchange for a couple of hours' volunteering a week.

'It's become a way for people in the area to get to know one another,' says Paul.

'We've got members who've lived in Elephant and Castle for many years mixing with those who've just moved into the fancy new developments.'

Mobile Gardeners moved here in May 2015, after their site on the Walworth Road came up for redevelopment. A community project on a low budget, this new garden is being established with recycled or donated materials.

Forklift truck pallets, scaffolding planks and old bike wheels have been inventively assembled into portable containers and are now home to *Verbena bonariensis* and *Leucanthemum vulgare*. An old toilet makes for another eccentric planter, while delivery crates rescued from the neighbouring construction workers are to be transformed to create the structure of a herbaceous border that will be tended by school and community groups.

All of it is parked on a space that, until just a few weeks ago, was nothing but rubble and dust.

RECIPE FOR RENEWAL

Harlem's Frederick Samuel Gardens is a multi-award winning community space that engages volunteers, youth groups and seniors in an urban beautification project whose roots run deep.

Every garden needs a *tour de force* and here Ms Blackwell is it. A long-time resident of 144th Street, one block away, she got tired of watching this plot waste to weed.

'It was my challenge to make it a flourishing green space,' she says. 'It took a lot of clearing and it took three years. But in our first year of opening we won first place in the NYCHA's citywide Manhattan vegetable contest, and the next year we did it again.'

The garden is now part of the New York City Housing Authority's (NYCHA's) Garden & Greening program, one the largest and oldest public gardening programmes in the USA. It has around 700 individual and community gardens in all five boroughs of NYC and approximately 3,500 participants annually.

Flowers, vegetables and friendship have all flourished in this award-winning community space in Harlem, New York City

The gardeners here grow food for public housing residents and they teach healthy eating to help improve lives in the low-income neighbourhood.

Their skill for maximising space in a constrained urban pitch is evident in the vertical planters packed with herbs and leafy greens, and the raised beds of burgeoning ornamentals.

Ms Blackwell is the leader of a dedicated bunch of 20, many of whom knew nothing about gardening when they joined the mission – an initiative of the Frederick Samuel Resident Association, which represents those living in public housing in the borough.

'They're learning as they go,' she says, 'but whatever their reason for being here, I insist that they eat the produce they grow or share it with someone in need. Everything here is about nutrition.'

It's an ethos that's helped stroke survivor Mr Wilson (pictured on page 84, far left), who visits most days: 'I made a mistake eating junk food and ended up on 26 different types of medication a day and in a wheelchair. I was depressed. I don't want to go through that again. I've changed my habits. I tell people healthy food is medicine. That's why the garden means a lot to me.'

To make the space work for as many people as possible, Ms Blackwell's volunteers have introduced small gardening plots and vertical planters that can be tended by individuals. Beds raised to waist height enable 'no bend' gardening for seniors, making 85-year-old Miss Mary 'the new flower girl' on site.

'I used to have a little yard when I lived in Long Island where I grew flowers. Flowers and colour are my thing; they're gifts from God,' says the retired caterer, tending the earth around her plants. 'I got involved as I needed more to do than sit around, watch television and go to Church.'

Once Ms Blackwell hooked her up with these planters, Miss Mary was unstoppable, planting 250 spring bulbs in two days. 'I'm old school. Once you commit yourself, you get on with it,' she laughs.

Lucia Moreira, mother of three, is another of Ms Blackwell's talented recruits. The space allows her to pass on what her grandmother, back in Guatemala, taught her.

'This is mint; we have seven types. You can boil it when you have a cold and drink it,' she says, snapping a leaf and holding it up. 'Here, smell it.'

Then, next to potatoes growing in an old laundry bin, she shows me clumps of the herb *Stevia rebaudiana*. 'We grow it for diabetic people. It's sweet but doesn't raise blood-sugar levels.'

At the end of a tour weaving between canes and around the foliage with Lucia, I have a bag full of produce to try – celery, raspberries, lime basil and coriander. The spirit of giving defines everything that is undertaken here.

But the generosity doesn't end with plants. Juan Carlos and son Adriene, here today to clear weeds from the paving cracks, are just two volunteers who've benefitted from the garden's tight social bonds.

'I was out of work and came to Ms Blackwell. She was there for me. She helped me fill in my job application and pointed me to somewhere she knew was hiring. I got work for a company that provides meals on wheels for elderly people. I'm now working full-time. She was there for me, she's there for everybody.'

I love the contrast between the bright, fresh *hosta* leaves and the rough, dark foliage of the *astilbe*.

HOW TO: MOBILE BOG GARDEN

If you want to create a garden that's on the move, you can't get better than the humble wheelbarrow to serve your needs. This is also a great solution if you do not have flowerbeds as it provides interesting planting space with a little bit of height. You can position other containers around your wheelbarrow and then easily rearrange them when you want to freshen up your display. When creating a bog garden there is no need for drainage holes since these plants like sitting in wet soil. I have chosen three moisture-loving plants – *Astilbe* 'Sprite', *Hosta* 'Wide Brim' and the royal fern (*Osmunda regalis*).

1. Pour a thin layer of coarse gravel into the bottom of the wheelbarrow.

2. Fill the wheelbarrow with good-quality topsoil or loam-based compost.

3. Remove your plants from their pots and place them so their base is level with the top of the wheelbarrow. Firm the soil around the roots.

4. Fill in around the plants with a good layer of mulch, such as well-rotted horse manure. A 5cm (2in) layer is ideal in this situation.

AFTERCARE & TIPS

Keep your bog garden topped up with water to ensure the soil stays moist and place it in part-shade. If you want to try this idea with plants that are suited to normal rather than boggy conditions, be sure to drill drainage holes in the bottom of the wheelbarrow to prevent their roots sitting in water.

Bog garden species to try: *Darmera peltata*, *Iris ensata* 'Variegata', candelabra primula species

This shoe-turned-plant-pot shows the myriad ways you can add your own personality to a garden. Make sure whatever receptacle you use has sufficient drainage holes so water can escape.

PROJECT RUNWAY

Photographer Jule Müller shares a rented apartment in Berlin's Neuköln neighbourhood with two girlfriends and a postage-stamp sized balcony.

When the flatmates stumbled upon a group of people who were building a communal garden at the abandoned Tempelhof airport, they immediately saw an opportunity to bring some much-needed outdoor space to their lives.

The Allmende Kontor Gemeinschaftsgarten provides 250 miniature garden plots for 500 space-constrained Berliners on the airfield-turned-public-park that surrounds the abandoned runway.

Established as a collective in 2011, the public is allowed to garden here for Ð30 to Ð60 year, depending on their income.

What is exciting is that even in their tiny spaces, plotholders can, and really do, impress their unique garden vision on the landscape.

Shoes, Barbie Doll heads and olive oil cans are made merry with plants of all kinds. There are 'rooftop' sun decks created from reclaimed wood, benches made from pallets and picket fences built with vinyl records.

'We asked if we could get involved, and they told us to just grab what we could find and build something of our own. We picked up some wood and nailed a plot together. It looked like a coffin but it did the job,' remembers Jule. 'I'm a child of the city. I've never had a garden before.'

As a beginner plot, and one of the first to be planted on the site, Jule's garden provides the flatmates with the perfectly sized space for a little no-fuss growing and a lot of experimentation.

This year they have *Eschscholzia californica*, *Melissa officinalis* and some lively *Eruca sativa* flopping over the sides of their raised bed. In the summer they bring friends and drinks, and hang out, picking and eating whatever is good that day.

Coming here daily to water gives Jule the chance to see another side of her native town: 'It's the only place in Berlin where you can see the sky. Whizzing along the runway on your bike towards the garden feels like freedom.'

Jule loves the informal approach at this community garden, where Berliners come to garden, party and hang out. 'We thought about signing up at the traditional allotments in the city but rigid rules mean you have to garden in a certain way.'

Concerns that the former airfield could contain chemicals, mean one of the site's few rules is that gardeners are not allowed to dig into the earth. Instead, they work with topsoil that is delivered. While the possibility of contaminants should not keep you from planting, it is important to undertake soil tests in places that have been used for industrial operations.

Guerrero Park, an 830m² (9,000ft²) garden, is one of Jane's latest efforts to introduce low-maintenance, hard-working gardens to the city.

SIDEWALK REVOLUTION

In San Francisco's garden scene, turning pavements into neat flower-filled spaces is an ever-popular pursuit. This is thanks to Jane Martin, who is on a one-women mission to green up bland surfaces to improve the health of San Francisco's streets and residents.

Ask San Francisco gardeners about Jane and they'll tell you she's a genius.

Over a decade ago, the artist and architect successfully persuaded City Hall to get serious about all the concrete around them.

San Francisco is a city where streets and public rights of way account for a quarter of its land area, and more than all the public parks combined. Quite simply, Jane believes that's wrong.

'I'd never lived in a place where public rights of way were so wide,' explains Jane, founder of Shift Design Studio. 'The default here is to pave the entirety, "wall to wall". But land has value. Cover it up and that's a lost opportunity.'

Her urge to green up the streets was welcomed by neighbours but didn't really take off until a hefty downpour of rain changed everything.

Jane employs low-impact materials, like these containers hewn from fallen tree logs and salvaged stainless-steel industrial heating ducts (opposite, below).

Planters made from logs of culled trees from Golden Gate Park support a diverse landscape of native and climate-adapted (drought-tolerant) plants, mimicking the natural ecological cycle of fallen trees in the wild supporting new life.

To enhance a public garden's durability, Jane avoids planting species with singular flowers and she also plants in irregular patterns. That way, if a flower gets picked or a plant is stolen or vandalised, the garden as a whole remains intact.

San Francisco's sewer system diverts wastewater and rain to a treatment plant but if the volumes are too high and too fast, water overwhelms the system. What happens next, as the city discovered in 2004, is that its low-lying areas become inundated with contaminated water.

During one such event, standing knee-deep in the flooded aftermath, Jane realised that sealed under a layer of concrete, the ground beneath her feet was dry – and that the garden she had created in the sidewalk outside her home could be part of a solution.

'I never intended to get into an environmental crusade,' says Jane, 'but it was clear that sidewalk gardens were a way to help address the overloaded system. Fortunately, the city was receptive to the message.'

The mayor directed city agencies to work with Jane to establish Sidewalk Landscape Permits, which allow citizens to green up patches of public space without paying an extortionate fee or thrashing about with an octopus of red tape.

'If living in the city is the most sustainable way to be on the planet, then the nicer we make that experience for people, the better,' explains Jane.

Jane's design skills are also in demand for the city's 'Pavement to Parks' programme, which turns superfluous roadway into places of recreation.

'The more connected you are to nature, even in a small way, the more sensitive you can be to decisions in your life that can affect it,' says Jane.

So many agree. Thousands of homeowners (see page 106), renters, businesses and schools in neighbourhoods across the entire city have applied for permits to undertake their own small-scale permeable landscaping projects, to get water and air into the soil, and create wildlife habitats and oxygen for streets.

Among them are volunteers in the Mission District, who were able to install a garden with hundreds of native and climate-adapted plants in a 31m (102ft) stretch of pavement.

A non-profit housing provider for the formerly homeless has also been able to create the first sidewalk landscape garden – of cordylines, *Dodonaea* and euphorbias – in the dense Tenderloin District.

Jane's non-profit outfit, Plant*SF, designs hard-working gardens as demonstrations. In a city with a year-round growing season that is in the clutches of an intense drought, this means using plants that have minimal water demands and do not need irrigation systems, while maximising the opportunities for abundant but low-impact gardens.

Though there are numerous positive outcomes from these all-new spaces, Jane gets most from seeing the human effect.

'The people who most appreciate sidewalk gardens are those whose daily life is comprised primarily of neighbourhood outings, like seniors with mobility issues who can't easily get to a destination park,' she observes. 'And little kids in tow on their parents' errands. Whatever's at their eye level is their world, so replacing barren concrete with abundant plantings changes their experience from one of fenders and tyres to an array of colours, textures and fragrances, all within arm's reach.

'They touch the plants with their eyes wide open.'

STREETSIDE STYLE

PAVEMENT PARADISE

Architect Lucy Marston is widely recognised for creating award-winning homes that have strong connections to their local context – physical, social, geographical and historical.

So when it came to designing the 15m² (160ft²) paved garden, at the front of her Edwardian home in east London's Haggerston, she naturally adopted a style that embraced how plants inhabit urban spaces, the way they opportunistically self-seed in any available chink in the concrete.

A 'lifeless' patio of Yorkstone paving was how Lucy describes the front of her home when she moved there in 2007.

Heavily pregnant with her second child and with the swift unpacking of boxes therefore a high priority, the space was in a state that suited the self-employed architect. But not for long. 'I found it frustrating living here and not having time to do something about the garden,' she says. 'I just had this urge to make it joyful.'

It seems that Londoners, more than most other city-dwellers we've visited for this book, shy from tackling their front gardens. Fear of vandalism and a perception that back gardens provide greater enjoyment and a higher reward-to-effort ratio are factors that are often mentioned. Lucy sees it differently: 'They're not often spaces where you spend much time. But the fact that you walk past them several times a day is why it's important to turn them into something. They create pleasure for yourself as well as for the street.'

As Lucy was beginning to consider the future for the front garden, she stuck a postcard advertising for help in the window of a Broadway Market café. Talented Lucy Conochie – our resident garden designer – spotted it and gave her a call.

It was a design match made in the Garden of Eden.

Lucy M wasn't seeking a makeover and she didn't want to get rid of the stone. Subtlety and a balance between the existing hardscaping and a new planting scheme were also integral to the design brief. Its wild style – with ethereal plants and wavy, loose textures – was Lucy C's idea.

Purple salvias, dusty pink poppies and lavender jostle with lime-green euphorbias and silvery-green artemisias. Since the garden was designed to evolve, prolific self-seeding plants such as *Linaria purpurea* were brought in, while wild campanulas – considered a weed by some and already resident in the well between the paving and basement window – were left alone. 'When the poppies dry, we shake the seedheads all over the place,' says Lucy M.

These plants have minimal water requirements and the paving keeps the ground beneath cool and moist, making this a low-maintenance, environmentally friendly garden.

Lucy's garden is full of purple and pink flowers that contrast beautifully with the bright greens: 'You can get away with a lot of green if you use different shades.'

Being a working mother of two, this looser vibe contained in distinct patches, met Lucy M's need for low maintenance.

'You can let wilder planting schemes grow for a long while before they need attention and if weeds appear, it isn't immediately obvious, like it is in a formal garden,' says Lucy C.

Easy-going grasses that require cutting once a year in early spring have been cleverly incorporated for that reason. But they also contrast with the stiffer, upright stems of plants such as *Verbena bonariensis*. Inspired by her visits to the informally styled Beth Chatto Gardens in Essex, Lucy M had an appetite for movement and feathery textures over clipped and neat.

This garden proves that a tinier than tiny patch, even if that's just a crack between the paving slabs, can offer so much. One unexpected consequence of this garden, in which the paving allows you to walk among the flora, is its effect on her children, Eddie and George.

'They've completely bought into it,' says Lucy M. 'I love the fact that the kids come out here now and that I do, too. Eddie lies on the paving stones looking at the plants and the insects while he's waiting to be taken to school. They both check enthusiastically on the plants – some of which they chose – and watch everything grow with interest.'

HOW TO: PLANTED PATIO GARDEN

To make even the hard landscaping in your garden vibrant with life, why not turn it into a planted patio garden? This is a really eco-friendly way of transforming a bit of old paving into a beautiful haven for insects, and it is quicker and cheaper than starting with new materials. A patio garden works particularly well if you have paving that has become a bit shabby, and where some of the slabs and mortar have cracked and broken. You can see these imperfections as planting opportunities. It is also a great solution in a front garden because it is low-maintenance and thief-proof, plus there's the added bonus that you'll be sharing your creation with the people who pass by.

Here I have used *Thymus* 'Archer's Gold', *Thymus* 'Purple Beauty' and *Sedum pluricaule* planted among some old Yorkstone paving.

1. Remove the old mortar or broken slab using a trowel or weeding hook. Take care to remove all the lumps and old concrete beneath the top surface.

2. Next, add a good helping of fresh, soil-based compost.

3. Using smaller plant specimens or plug plants means that you can bring plant life even to the smallest gaps. Place your plant and firm the compost around the root ball.

4. Add a layer of horticultural grit as an attractive finish that also keeps in moisture and improves drainage around the base of the plants.

AFTERCARE & TIPS

Choosing drought-tolerant plants is a good start; many culinary herbs are in this category. Species that self-seed prolifically will add yet another dynamic element to your planting, finding their way into the cracks in the paving and producing a different effect every year.

Other plants to try: Mexican fleabane (*Erigeron karvinskianus*), *Lychnis coronaria*, *Origanum majorana*, *Thymus* 'Silver Queen', *Verbena bonariensis*

PARKLET LIFE

Kimberly Conley and Deep Jawa created San Francisco's very first residential parklet at the front of their Victorian home in the city's Mission District in 2011. Parklets are small parks created in pavement space, funded privately but designed for and used by the public.

Thanks to the making of the 'Deepistan National Parklet', salvias, alyogynes, cycads, iris, wisteria and Trixie, a succulent topiary dinosaur, have all arrived on Valencia Street, a busy thoroughfare between trendy coffee houses and fashionable boutiques.

But Deepistan has brought much else besides – impromptu musical gigs, hummingbirds, toddlers bearing gifts and a first-class showcase of eco-friendly urban garden design.

'The space used to be hideous,' says Kimberly, referring to the old slab of concrete they lived with previously.

It sometimes provided a place for barbecues, and usually functioned as a route to the garage but Deep, who lived here before he met Kimberly, always knew it could be so much more.

Not just prettier and more enjoyable, but offering a space for wider communal benefit, too.

Deepistan's colour scheme is sympathetic to the house and nearby buildings, creating a cohesive effect. Iris, wisteria and silvery purple senecio provide different shades of purple, varying the tones.

Deep and Kim's parklet has been so successful that they say they'd build one wherever they lived next. 'A driveway is such a horrible waste in a space-constrained city,' says Deep. The eco-aware couple doesn't own a car, instead travelling the city by bicycle, foot and public transport.

'Valencia Street is such a great street, a place where people like to hang out. And I always spent lots of time out there, working on projects on the driveway. But I hated the space,' remembers Deep. 'Part of the idea of parklets is to highlight the spaces our society unthinkingly reserves for cars.'

In a city where public rights of way are so widespread, rethinking the relationship between traffic and pedestrians is, for inventive types like this pair, a perfect opportunity for aesthetic landscaping and a way to address pressing environmental issues along the way.

Enter Jane Martin, architect and artist (see page 94), who runs Shift Design Studio. Deep contacted Jane for help and the pavement's destiny was set.

Then came Kimberly. 'When I met Deep he was working on this vision and I was super-excited. I love gardening. Living in small apartments in cities, I'd only been able to have a window box. So I got my wish for a garden,' she says of the 21m² (226ft²) plot.

Kimberly is therefore the 'Deepistan Park Ranger', carefully tending Jane's plant selections. Though Deepistan is definitely not high-maintenance. 'That wasn't the intention,' explains Kimberly. 'We have climate-appropriate plants that don't require lots of water or nutrients. That was absolutely a design priority for us.'

Yucca, *Dietes*, convolvulus and senecio were bedded in to give Deepistan an unexpected drought-tolerant character – lush and abundant despite being water-wise.

Native plants such as the blue-flowering shrub, *Ceanothus*, and *Gaura*, a bright, generously-flowering perennial, also make for a garden that is more suited to this environment, reducing demands on resources and ensuring the plants are more likely to survive.

Jane advised they bring in an artistic focal point, too and this resulted in Trixie the Triceratops. She was crafted from a metal frame armature with mesh, dirt, and a plant substrate, and then completed with a layer of *Sedum dasyphyllum* 'Minor' to create the skin. Topping it all are three hand-hewn redwood horns.

The inclusion of cycads in the parklet, a prehistoric plant species that has persisted to the present day, is a nod to the foliage that would have been eaten by Trixie's ancestors.

Trixie was an instant hit. 'Kids come by and leave toys for her. People put flowers on her horns,' says Deep, whose childhood fascination with dinosaurs was behind the concept. 'She's the garden's identity. She lends it personality.'

Seating was an important feature to get right, too. Passers-by must realise the garden is public but must not be so comfortable that they outstay their welcome. Parklet etiquette is that you come, eat ice cream, read or enjoy the flowers, and then move on. Benches, therefore, are extensions of the containers, while spaces for leaning encourage fleeting stays.

There are, inevitably in any public space, annoyances. Namely graffiti. Jane's idea was to use easy-to-clean aluminium for planters and to help combat trouble, to employ plants that hang over the surfaces facing the approaching foot traffic. 'Graffiti happen but rarely. Although it's irritating, it's nothing compared to the happiness that Deepistan has brought us,' explains Deep.

That happiness comes from the unplanned encounters, an unexpected pleasure for the naturally more reserved Kimberly, who's learnt to enjoy the fact that living with a parklet means you are often greeted by smiling, curious strangers.

Pragmatism, as well as low water and nutrient use, was a key consideration in the planting scheme. Extremely hot conditions and high footfall from people and dogs relieving themselves necessitated the use of tough urban species, like this robust Borago officinalis.

'Typically a garden is at the back of the house and growing up, that was what I was used to – not a public gathering space. So this has been a fantastic experience for me because it's changed my whole view that a garden is something you cultivate just for yourself,' she says.

Out in the garden they find thank-you notes in the containers, musicians making music and visitors who've dropped by to proudly show their grandchildren or friends from out of town the spectacular spot in the sidewalk.

'Deep really makes the most of that social element,' says Kimberly. 'When the World Cup was on, he took a TV down there and made some good friends that way. It's really opened up our home. I wouldn't ever have thought I'd enjoy a front garden so much.'

Big planters give the garden street scale and are unapologetically bold, balancing the physical presence of cars. The large volume of soil they contain reduces the need for watering.

Tall planters put the plants at eye-level, making their colour, scent and texture more accessible, particularly to children. 'You get a close-up experience and can see all the bugs and birds that visit the flowers,' says Deep.

Kathy's husband Drew and son Doug (opposite) are caretakers of the beautiful Californian garden she created.

Don't be afraid of planting tall plants in small gardens. As well as providing visual interest, they can be used to block an unsightly view.

California poppies (above) quickly lay down mats of foliage and have low-watering needs.

MINI MEADOW

Kathy Russell's front yard, in Brentwood, west Los Angeles, had never been much to capture the imagination. Like many of her neighbours in this leafy street, the garden comprised a water-hungry lawn, a lonely camellia and two black acacia trees. But when Kathy retired from her job as a surgical nurse, she decided it was time to turn it into something good.

Environmentally savvy, Kathy understood what a 'good' garden could mean – drought-tolerant plants, species for wildlife and plants native to California's Mediterranean climate.

To get this all just right, Kathy was diligent in her research. She took out books from the library and marked suitable pages with Post-it notes. She took classes on horticulture and went on garden tours. And eventually, she teamed up with sustainable landscape designer, Shayne Naudi, to help develop her ideas.

Her planning took a year: Kathy was determined. So much so that she colonised a strip of sidewalk at the front of her house as part of her project.

First came a fence, then a drip irrigation system calibrated for species with low-water needs. Then, the native plants that possessed the desired romantic effect arrived.

Dreamy, insect-loving *Achillea millefolium* 'Sonoma Coast' and mounds of fragrant *Verbena lilacina* 'De La Mina' for butterflies took position in borders. And to soften the kerbstones, Kathy planted masses of white-to-pink flowered *Erigeron karvinskianus* – another bee and butterfly temptress.

Brimming with wildlife and ethereal forms that shift in the wind, this is a garden that moves. It also envelops. Facing it front on you can barely see the Russell house behind the sidewalk, which is a waist-high meadow of trumpet-shaped *Mimulus aurantiacus*, carex grasses and San Diego sunflower (*Viguiera laciniata*).

Thoughtfully designed as a garden of healing and a refuge for creatures, when Kathy became ill, it turned into her refuge, too. 'Even when she wasn't feeling up to it, she made a point of coming out to the garden as much as she could,' says her son Doug, who lives next door. 'I have lovely memories of seeing her out there during that time.'

Kathy was far too modest to consider the garden would be of interest to anyone other than herself. But in March 2015, a year after she died, hundreds visited it as part of the Theodore Payne Native Plant Garden Tour, an annual tour of 35 of the region's most beautiful and inspiring public and private landscapes. 'It was a tribute to her and I'm so pleased we did it,' says her husband Drew. 'People absolutely loved it.'

NURTURING
NOOKS

CREATIVE SPARK

When London firefighter Simon Jakeman began to find himself and colleagues battling on the front line of climate change, he decided it was time to try and make a difference, so he set about rescuing the roof at Surbiton Fire Station from moss-covered emptiness. Today it is a lush space that has inspired many others to green up their own concrete boxes for the good of the planet.

The moment you step into the grounds of Surbiton Fire Station, recently crowned London's greenest, it is immediately clear that someone's been very busy.

There are upturned helmets transformed into hanging baskets, plants bursting from recycled car tyres and buckets, a bird box nailed to a tree trunk and flowers themed in the fire station's 'watch' colours of blue, white, red and green.

Up on the roof, pots, packed tight into every nook, flaunt *Centaurea cyanus*, lobelias and alliums, geraniums, tomatoes and a fig tree. And there are bees – lots of them.

Simon's colleagues tease that TV celebrity gardener Alan Titchmarsh had a hand in all this but they well know that the Ground Force behind this garden is Simon alone.

'One year was really wet and there were slugs everywhere. So we put a pond in for the frogs because I didn't want to use slug pellets. Slug numbers went down. You learn so much,' says Simon.

Walls absorb heat making them ideal places to locate plants that like warmth. Strawberries still grow here in January because of the heat of the wall.

'We're the ones out there dealing with the effects of climate change,' he says. 'We've been called to more and more climate change-related incidents, such as flooding. One day I just thought, let's do something to help, even if it's just in a very small way.'

His original ambition back in 2011 was to plant for insects, to sow pollen-rich flower mixes for bees and buddleja for butterflies. But soon after came the robins and blackbirds. Then endangered species like stag beetles, and a frog ('probably via a bag of compost,' he admits). And then came school groups, cub scouts, MPs and local councillors.

As the word spread, others began to wild their own spaces with fervour – the courtyard of the local environment centre, along the high street, and before too long, Simon hopes, other patches of empty ground.

'This garden is here to get the message out there,' he says. 'Locals come and visit and then go back home and do it themselves.' The Mayor liked the idea so much that the roof garden features in the London Fire Brigade's sustainability plan.

Simon's tiny garden, as they say, went viral.

'We've got to join everything together. Lots of small efforts here and there really do add up to make a big difference,' he says.

What's remarkable is that all this influence has been mastered without any budget at all. Relying solely on donations, the fire fighter has created a green haven across the 72m^2 (775ft^2) of roof. Prize money, from competitions and awards, goes straight into buying seeds and plug plants.

'That, over there, was a box we kept sand in that was heading for the skip. And a friend gave me that water feature,' says Simon, who tends the rooftop while he's off duty.

With the sun on the spot until mid-afternoon, the rooftop is a fruitful place and produces most of the vegetables – onions, leeks and Brussels sprouts – for the fire fighters' Christmas dinner. The south-facing wall at the back, which absorbs heat during the day and releases it through the night, promotes the ripening of apples and strawberries.

'The bees love it. The birds love it. The garden has totally changed the atmosphere of this place,' says Simon, whose passion for gardening was inspired by his grandfather.

This microclimate is also perfect for the resident olive tree, which hails from the sunny Mediterranean. Trees around the grounds beneath also shelter the space from high winds, protecting the plants from drying out, which containerised plants are particularly vulnerable to.

Out on the roof, where Simon now spends his downtime 'rather than sitting indoors watching TV', he can't help but turn his mind to the flat, empty roof of the library two doors down. 'I'm always thinking to myself "that one should be next",' says the winner of the WWF's 2013 Hidden Hero award.

If Simon has anything to do with it, it's only a matter of time.

1. Start by filling the base of the gabion with a mixture of pebbles, keeping the largest ones along the outside to prevent the smaller ones dropping through the mesh.

2. Lay hessian in the middle of the pebble bed and start to fill with soil. This will provide a root zone for the plants.

HOW TO: GABION INSECT GARDEN

Create a home for garden minibeasts without compromising on contemporary style with this planted gabion basket. Gabions are wire mesh cages designed to hold a range of hard materials. Here I have filled my gabion with pebbles to create valuable hiding places for insects and spiders, and I have created wild and wispy planting on top to attract yet more critters to this tiny space. Encouraging beneficial insects to your garden is very important, especially if you like to grow organically, since many of these creatures will feed on garden pests such as aphids. What is more, supporting a range of insect life means you will attract more birds to your plot. I have used a simple mix of *Linaria purpurea* 'Canon Went', *Koeleria glauca* 'Coolio' and Mexican feather grass (*Stipa tenuissima*), which contrasts well with the pebbles and sways in the gentlest of breezes.

3. Build up layers of pebbles around and under the hessian, filling with soil as you go and making sure the hessian is not visible from the outside.

4. Lay the lid down and mark out where you want your planting hole to be. Wearing leather gloves, cut out a hole in the lid with bolt-cutters.

5. Fix the lid to the sides using spiral fasteners to wind around the joins.

6. Take your plant out of its pot and remove any dead or damaged leaves. Place the plant and firm the soil around the root ball. I chose to plant quite closely for maximum effect.

7. Cover the top layer with slightly smaller pebbles, taking care not to damage the base of the plants.

AFTERCARE & TIPS

Customise your gabion to suit your style by using different materials such as slices of wood, coloured pieces of rock or slate. If you don't fancy planting the top of your gabion, it can double-up as a garden seat. Gabions usually come flat-packed, either with handy clips for assembly, or with spiral fasteners like the ones I used here. Your supplier should make sure that you have everything you need to assemble yours.

Insect-friendly plants to try: *Calamintha nepeta*, *Origanum vulgare*, *Salvia nemorosa* 'Caradonna'

Plants at different heights will cater to a range of organisms, while making insect-damage, such as gnawed leaves, less obvious.

The tiny gardens pictured are some of the many Elisa has designed in San Francisco.

FORCE OF NATURE

Elisa Baier thinks tiny for a living. Founder and principal of San Francisco-based outdoor design firm, Small Spot Gardens, she creates intimate gardens in city-sized spaces, believing that gardens can make lives richer, healthier and happier – whatever the garden's dimensions.

Feeling exasperated over the awkward, boring outdoor space in your life? Take heart: there's a cure. A ten-minute dose of this ebullient lady and you'll no longer doubt the infinite potential for beauty that is just waiting in your back yard.

Elisa is evangelical about helping city-dwellers grow deep roots into nature. Let other designers roll out mundane visions of paradise. Elisa has a different dream. 'I'm constantly surprised at what people want out of their small spaces,' she says. 'Often they just want gardens to be easy and clean. My role is to get people excited about what they could be. Designing gardens should be about bringing nature into a person's life, mentally and physically.'

Elisa began working on her mission in 2010, with no more than a pushbike, a 'weed whacker' and a small client book of friends-of-friends. Small Spot Gardens was established with the deliberate aim of reaching city residents whose plots and budgets were both constrained.

But news of Elisa's healing powers swiftly spread and she now employs a five-strong team to serve the overwhelming demand from those in need of help with spaces of up to 95m^2 (1,000ft^2).

'There's something really powerful about how plants do their thing and will continue to with or without us,' says Elisa.

It's okay that Elisa's clients don't have oodles of cash to invest: she wants her work to be as accessible as possible to the average person living in the city. Her motivation is to make San Francisco's back yards as environmentally useful as they are decorative – and the more she can get her hands on, the better.

A botanist by training, Elisa is excited about the potential that the combined impact of a city's tiny green islands could, and does, have on its ecology and wider health. Rain gardens – small areas that allow rainwater runoff from impervious surfaces like roofs – sidewalk gardens, gardens on a roof – they all make an invaluable contribution to the greater environmental good.

'Cities are more and more crowded and because of that, accessing wilderness is becoming more difficult for those living in urban areas,' explains Elisa, who also teaches small-scale garden skills. 'So our little spaces are increasingly important.'

Her micro gardens – such as those pictured – are therefore strongly influenced by plant biology and ecosystem science. Elisa, who grew up playing in the woodlands near her home in Madison County, NY, rightly views diminutive spaces as vibrant living systems in their own right. Tiny plot owners, she argues, should pay as much heed to soil organisms as any gardener. Worms, nematodes, root bacteria and a billion other creatures besides can live in just one tablespoon of earth. 'Crazy huh,' she marvels.

'What happens underground is amazing,' she continues. 'An urban garden is part of a fascinating and complicated metropolitan ecosystem. By working with natural processes, your garden can clean air, filter polluted runoff and help wildlife.'

Elisa recommends that gardeners work with the tones and materials of an outdoor space to create a holistic effect. Here the fence is complemented by wooden deck chairs, keeping the look uniform.

The more types of plants, the more types of roots you have in your soil and the healthier it is, as they produce a wider array of beneficial soil organisms.

Mulch, compost and groundcover plants that retain soil moisture and provide food for organisms to eat are therefore integral to her design practices. Above ground, she avoids chemical sprays for the harm they do to insects.

Elisa's gardens are created in an 'urban natural' style. Clean lines created by borders and benches and containers in rustic textures and materials are teamed with an abundant and diverse range of plants that offer textural focal points. Colourful or recycled garden accessories – such as ceramic planters or reclaimed furniture – are often also part of the compositional mix. 'My approach is defined by diverse, dense planting and geometric angles. It makes my eye happy because the space is better organised,' she says. 'Appealing designs are those that have plants flowing over edges and then clean lines to keep them in check.'

But there is soul-searching to be done before tackling any of this. Anyone looking at renovating a garden, she advises, should start with the 'super-practical questions' about how they will use that space. 'Think about your basic needs. Do you have pets? Do you have children? Do you have the sun? If so, where is it? Do you have privacy issues? When you've decided all of that, then think about style,' she reveals.

Owners of tiny spaces often feel compelled to make a space feel bigger, but Elisa instead encourages creating a feeling of intimacy and retreat by using layering. Incorporating low garden walls to create different rooms and maximise tiny areas are one way of doing this, she says: 'Often on paper that feels scary, like it might make a space more claustrophobic, but it has the opposite effect.'

Getting the best out of your design is also about balance. 'A limited colour scheme in a small space is incredibly important, and may be the most important design rule,' she says. Elisa advises on using two to three contrasting foliage colours, and flowers for brief 'punches' of colour.

'People run to the store on the first day of spring and buy every single plant they like. Such a bad idea,' she laughs. 'You have to control yourself!' Instead, Elisa advises to buy five or six types of plants but about three to five of each, which is also brilliant if you're on a low budget. 'Clump them in groups and then, when you can afford it, buy more of the same plant. Buying multiples establishes a pattern and once you've got that, you can pop in some favourites as single plants.'

Feeling better? Told you it would only take ten minutes.

Lucy kept a vegetable plot in this border but replaced it with these captivating ornamentals (opposite). 'I'm more interested in seeing how plants grow together. Vegetables can work well in containers, though, and don't take up valuable space. And tomato plants are fine in pots.'

WILD IN WALTHAMSTOW

My Tiny Garden's very own **Lucy Conochie is an award-winning garden designer whose London-based practice is fast gaining a reputation for its innovative and imaginative gardens. With a passion for wild and natural environments she advocates a naturalistic planting style and simple use of materials.**

It is in the small terrace garden of her Walthamstow home, which she shares with husband Benjamin Doherty, where Lucy experiments with new ideas, plant combinations and colour, resulting in an energetic garden that is a feast for wildlife.

Lucy and Ben have been renting this house for just over three years. When the estate agent showed them around the back garden they were confronted with little more than a giant cherry tree, a tangle of roots, rubble, rubbish and deep shade.

It was, as Lucy describes, an 'awful garden' but a tantalising blank canvas. So, out came the ungainly shrubs, the cherry tree and the rubbish, leaving a ten-year-old elder that kept its place thanks to Lucy's love of weeds and its pleasing shape. In came a small retaining wall and a lawn, as part of a cultivation job that took over a year to complete.

And that's when the experiment began.

Allium sphaerocephalon's flowers (right) turn from green to pink and will gently self-sow.

'You get told when you're training to be a garden designer that you shouldn't let your garden become a test bed. I don't agree with that,' reveals Lucy. 'I like having the opportunity to try out plant combinations and layouts, and I don't mind that it isn't a fully rounded concept from the outset. A garden is in motion all the time; you can't stop it changing. A garden is impactful because of the plants, not because you sit down and decide to follow a rule.'

Laying the circular lawn made an instant impact but it has since shrunk as the plant borders became increasingly generous. Her current pride and joy is a 'riotous' border of grasses, poppies, alliums, sedums and echinaceas, which provide colour in summer and attractive structural interest in winter. 'The border is our main view from the house so I wanted it to be tall, mad and visually appealing throughout the year,' she says.

She planted a woodland garden under the elder with shade-tolerant plants such as the hart's tongue fern, *Brunnera macrophylla* and an acer. 'Other things I planted just to see what happened,' says Lucy cheerfully. A *Rodgersia* 'Herkules', generally happy in moist woodland areas, is straining for the light and needs moving. 'It's easy to lose perspective when you're choosing plants but one tip is to imagine yourself as the plant and look up at the light it will receive. That helps you understand whether the location will be suitable.'

Among the principles Lucy does hold dear is to plant what the insects love: 'It seems right to me. That's what a flower is for, it's their function. I don't like over-cultivated plants that are superficial or for show. Their beauty leaves a bad taste in the mouth when you realise a bee can't access the pollen because the flowers are too densely packed.'

Lucy never uses chemical fertilisers, instead preferring to nurture the soil with home-made organic feeds of comfrey and nettles.

Blue-flowered *Pulmonaria officinalis*, and the long racemes of the pink-flowered *Linaria purpurea* are just two of the plants on the menu for the bees in this garden.

Another of Lucy's recommendations is to accept what you have and not fight the natural conditions of a space. Terraced gardens are often fraught with tough conditions – shade from buildings, trees and fences, and dry soil conditions. 'They're often like woodland environments, so a good rule is to go for plants that live on the edges of woodlands as they can cope with conditions near fences, for instance,' she says, as a Red Admiral butterfly flits by. 'If you embrace the environment, your rewards will be much greater. There's a plant for every situation.'

Heavily influenced by Dutch garden architect, Henk Gerritsen, who believed in respecting the full life cycle of the garden, Lucy believes weeds can be an essential part of a garden's beauty. 'You could spend your life eradicating a plant because it disrupts your plans. But you could also decide to let it grow and appreciate its form,' she says.

Lucy, who hails from a family of enthusiastic gardeners, cannot remember a time when she did not garden. Even as a nomadic art student, roaming from one house to the next, she would create gardens in every place, buying plants on her way home from college and beautifying whatever space she had. 'People would ask "why bother when you're only there for a year?" But it never occurred to me not to do it.'

One plant that has travelled along with her since she left home 16 years ago is the *Salix babylonica* var. *pekinensis* 'Tortuosa' (opposite, above right), which grew in her childhood garden. That specimen was itself a cutting from her grandmother's tree.

'It would be twice the size if I hadn't moved it so often, poor thing,' says Lucy. 'It's not particularly glam but it's close to my heart because of that connection. I love the way it moves, too.'

'It's one of the first plants to bud in spring. It makes me happy.'

SOULS ENTWINED

**Adrian Card is a painter who specialises in furniture, murals and harpsichords. Years spent
living in shared apartments in San Francisco sparked a fascination with the creative possibilities
that the texture and colour of a garden – no matter how small or temporary – could illuminate.**

**When he met John Tinker, a creative writing professor at Stanford University, in 1990, he found
a kindred gardener's spirit. They fell in love and moved into a ramshackle house that possessed
the garden project of their dreams – one that was to become intimately entwined in the path
that their lives subsequently followed.**

We were urged to visit Adrian's garden by other gardeners in the city. His 1850s house, set back
from the road, is considered old in a city that lies on a fault line. Situated in the neighbourhood of
Bayview, the house rests on a history that is deep. Abundant water, fog and the sunniest weather
in the city seduced settlers of centuries past to raise flower crops from its fertile earth.

Adrian's garden sounded rare and beautiful. In our correspondence he'd mentioned a serpentine
brick pathway of calla lilies, tree ferns and Mexican palms on one side of the house. Since corridors
like this are typically overlooked, our curiosity was piqued by the ingenuity that such an awkward
plot could inspire.

'April is a good time to see it,' wrote Adrian. 'In the morning it's shady but in the afternoon, the
sun illuminates it beautifully. Do come.'

*Citrus (opposite, above right) can
be grown in containers but must be
moved to a cool, frost-free, bright
environment – like a sunny windowsill
– during the winter.*

*Repeating colour at regular intervals
(opposite, below right) gives rhythm.*

Undulating, wavy leaf textures echo the curvature of the pathway (far right) but they also cleverly contrast with the hard brick.

Vibrant coloured plants provide focal points. Place them next to taller plants or structures to maintain balance, as Adrian has done here with this Aloe maculata (opposite, above).

Pebbles of recycled glass (below right) create a subtle backdrop for the dramatic palm tree.

So, on a bright spring day, I headed for Bayview, eager to meet the lovely man we'd been writing to for months.

Indeed, the 3-m (10-ft) wide snaking pathway, created to 'draw eyes and feet to the back garden', was, indeed, special. Despite its journeying purpose it was distinct from the wild romance of the foxgloves and rose behind the house. Lush swords and swirls of foliage were packed into its borders, their deep greens puncturing the diffuse light. It was an adventure in the exotic.

Sprays of *Dianella tasmanica*, which grows in Australian forests, have been planted for their vivid violet-blue berries, like beads of glass. 'Don't they look both real and unreal?' said Adrian. A plant for shade or partial shade, and a warm sheltered position, it is perfect here by the wall.

These otherworldly colour bursts were echoed at the path's end, where pebbles of multi-coloured glass were spread about a U-shaped bed, brimming with succulents.

After our tour around the back, Adrian showed me a stack of typed notes. They had barely been shared since they were completed. I placed a handful of lemons he'd picked for me on the kitchen table, and leafed through.

'I imagine the tremendous forces always taking place in my tiny swatch of ground, the seeds, the blooms ... the bursts of fecundity, the appetites of plants and critters, the unstoppable vigour of garden life just outside my bedroom window,' John wrote in 2010.

It was eight years before that when John and Adrian had begun to imagine the tropical brick pathway, the succulent garden and their 'meadow fantasy' of foxgloves and poppies. And then they made it real. At their wedding a friend spoke of how the couple had created a space of enchanting fantasy.

When John's cancer became too severe to work, he spent every day in their garden. But he continued to write. The loose sheets Adrian was sharing were a memoir of the garden from which he distilled sense from the chaos of his body.

Artfully displayed pots are a great trick for small spaces, indoors or outdoors. Placing containers at varying heights draws attention to their decorative features.

'If I could draw forth from the garden an abundant, luscious, graceful and vigorous environment, I could imagine that I was drawing forth the same within my body,' he explained.

In one entry he reflected that to think of one's garden as home was 'pretty wacky' given it was a 'place of change attuned to the cycle of the seasons, the changes of weather, a space to be negotiated with so many other living beings.' Despite that: 'I'm ready to engage with the garden like this because I don't watch TV ... [or] run a Facebook account.'

He preferred to focus on the living things around him.

John's insights into what nature can effect are true, whatever space it appears in, and it inspires creativity even when creativity feels out of reach.

As John wrote weeks before he died: 'The garden lives through cycles. Each fall the herbaceous plants die back, some to the ground. Some reseed, some simply decline, only to grow and thrive again ... Some plants return nearly identically in the next round of seasons, some simply won't be seen again. It's the gardener's task and joy to control that tension between wild growth and a cultivated designed environment.

'I learn to trust in change, in the spirit of transformation.'

DELIGHTS IN SHADE

Owning a shady space
doesn't mean you
have to be boring.
Use bold plants to
bring character.
Architectural plants
that are happy
in shade include
Fatsia japonica *and*
Trachycarpus.

HEART OF PALM

Jared Braiterman is a man with exotic tastes and a love of warm weather. His light-starved back yard in Clinton Park, San Francisco, with its cool, mild summers and sea fog, was no natural bedfellow for plants from the Mediterranean. But in spite of the weather, Jared has curated an energetic garden with the personality of summer.

And it's been thriving for almost two decades.

After he'd torn out the concrete staircase and levelled the 32m² (345ft²) back yard with a circle-shaped border at its centre, Jared stood with his hands on his hips and wondered what to do next.

The forest of statuesque trees that surrounded the boundary of this garden-to-be cast shade here for most of the day and made growing food crops out of the question. The sun-worshipping lemon tree he'd tried had withered miserably.

A friend and palm-tree enthusiast suggested he give a King palm tree, (*Archontophoenix cunninghamiana*), a whirl because of its tolerance of partial shade. A compact *Pritchardia* that could cope with miserable summers and was native to Hawaii's rainy regions was the next experiment.

Palms, it seemed, were working, so Jared sourced more – from brokers, hobbyists and palm fanatics. And then they started to appear out front, too. Queen palms, whose lacy deep green fronds can reach up to 15m (50ft), started to occupy sidewalk planters.

This tropical back yard is now Jared's 'favourite' room in the house he has shared with husband Shu since 1999. Brightening the space with jewels of colour are pale yellow clivias, red fuchsias, purple-and-white passifloras, plus a philadelphus, which produces creamy white flowers and an orange-blossom perfume.

'I'm here all the time, morning and night, taking care of something or other,' says Jared, whose grandmother inspired his green fingers. 'I work out here and play music out here,' he says, as a portly bumble bee crosses our path. 'The garden's a companion, a relaxing space. It is something to live alongside. There are people who love pets but for me, it's plants. It's a connection to something alive and changing.'

Indoors, he's been equally inventive with the constraints of the space. The pocket gardens he's created between the side of his house and his neighbours' exterior walls demonstrate his no-nonsense approach to gardens of small proportions.

Jared has installed windows on the part of the walls that face into the kitchen and bathroom, revealing the columns of space left between this house and the next – typical features between homes in the city to boost air circulation.

The results are like display cases. 'People usually keep these spaces empty but I wanted more greenery and the challenge of growing something everywhere,' explains Jared.

Part of these quirky displays is bamboo, gunning for a position sky-side of the roof, while to create interest at eye-level, zebra plants (*Aphelandra squarrosa*), with their emerald-and-white leaves, have been planted as specimens that are suited to indirect light.

Similarly, on the wall of the lounge, where you might expect a painting, is a large rectangular window that reveals an artful tangle of foliage growing on the other side. Defined by splashes of the bright red-orange lanterns of *Physalis alkekengi*, it is a modern masterpiece in its own right. It is lit up at night.

'The idea was to feel like you're in the garden when you're indoors. I planted anything I thought would grow and it's taken a lot of experimentation. There are lots of things that don't work and you never know why. I like to combine a bit of planning with an attitude of just letting it all happen. Gardening is so much more fun that way,' he grins.

This garden's personality is evident everywhere, including in this fun and brightly-coloured bird box (opposite, above). Position objects of interest like this in the light so they can be seen.

'This is my centre, my place to come back to. It is a companion, a relaxing space and a living creature,' says Jared, who divides his time between San Francisco and Tokyo (see page 10).

Maidenhair ferns (opposite, below) are ideal in shady gardens but need high humidity. Place in pots on a layer of pebbles and mist frequently.

145

ENTREPRENEUR'S EDEN

Lucas Badtke-Berkow runs a publishing and media agency with his wife, Kaori Sakurai. Knee High Media is an ultra-cool company that is known for its unique take on culture. It is also the brains behind Japan's most influential magazines. And Lucas and Kaori's garden grows as a forest of inspiration.

Amid the dappled light in the back yard of their home and office in Tokyo's Shibuya-ku district, Lucas and Kaori grow plants that fire the imagination.

This small woodland garden, which dwells under an old persimmon tree, is a limitless landscape.

Lucas, who has been making magazines since he was 16, launched *Planted* in Japan in 2006 with the slogan 'Life with plants on this planet'. 'Nature is a big part of our magazines because it's a big part of culture,' he says. 'You can't understand culture without talking about nature.'

This garden, therefore, feeds the stories that happen on the pages of the magazines that the team, who work on the second floor of this old house, lovingly creates. Titles such as *Tokion*, *Papersky* and *Mammoth* take plants as seriously as they do history, travel or fashion – exploring the myriad ways that plants are entwined in the cultural consciousness. There's a purple passiflora growing in one corner. Known as 'the clock plant' in Japan,

Plants growing under trees can be difficult to establish as they tend to be starved of moisture, light and nutrients. Lucas has planted a Fatsia japonica, *which can thrive despite the shadow cast by trees and buildings.*

Basil 'Dolce Fresca', specially bred in this garden, went on to win the 2015 All-America Best Vegetable Seed Award.

Ivy (opposite, right) makes a great climber or shrub for walls and fences that receive little sunlight. Hedera helix 'Caecilia' is compact and can be grown in a container.

it inspired a feature in kid's magazine, *Mammoth*, that explored the concept of time. A new cultivar of basil, 'Dolce Fresca', was specially bred in this garden to support a healthy eating campaign.

Lucas and Kaori sleep beneath the deck of their media operation. Their bedroom, which opens onto the garden, is kitted out with a futon and lanterns, and is designed as a campsite under the stars. A motif of pebbles begins with a patterned rug at the bedroom door and continues outdoors with a stone pathway to the pond, bringing the garden indoors.

On summer days there are apple mint and pineapple mint for iced teas, and a chestnut-brown flowered morning glory that was bred in Edo times

(1603–1868). But it is white-flowered species that dominate – *Gardenia jasminoides* and *Hibiscus syriacus* 'Diana' – keeping the palette cool and simple in the tropical Tokyo heat.

Being so close to the space, the couple sought species that would lend a sense of enchantment all year round. A late-flowering cherry tree, 'Yaezakura', whose blossom arrives just as most across Tokyo wither, has a place here because, as Lucas says, 'After those trees are done you get sad'. A jasmine planted for its scent sprawls the garden wall. The pond has been created for the power that the presence of water can bring about.

Small and shady it may be, but this is a national park of ideas.

HOW TO: TINY POND GARDEN

Building a pond is one of the best ways to encourage wildlife to your garden, and it is incredibly restful to sit and watch the water on a lazy afternoon. This old whisky barrel is fantastic for a rustic look. Its wooden slats cleverly swell when the barrel is filled with water, making it completely watertight. Even a tiny pond such as this one will be host to a wide range of insects and other invertebrates. Birds will also find it invaluable as a source of water during dry weather. If you want to invite amphibians to stay, you can sink your barrel into the ground so the rim is close to ground level. Ponds need a good range of plant life to keep the water healthy, so make sure you have underwater oxygenating weeds, something to provide surface cover such as a water lily, and some marginal plants such as bogbean (*Menyanthes trifoliata*) or water forget-me-not (*Myosotis scorpioides*).

1. Start by potting up your aquatic plants in larger baskets to give them room to grow. Line each basket with a hessian square.

2. Add a little aquatic compost to the bottom and then place your plant in, having removed any dead or damaged leaves. Here I am using *Equisetum hyemale*.

3. Fill in the gaps with the aquatic compost, making sure to leave enough room for gravel on top.

4. Then, firm the compost in well so there are no air pockets.

5. Add a layer of gravel or pea shingle to completely cover the compost. This prevents it all washing away into the water.

6. Set the baskets in the barrel and build them up with bricks so the tops of the marginal plants sit about 10cm (4in) below the rim of the barrel. The water lily favours deep water so it does not need bricks.

7. I needed about three layers of bricks to raise my marginal plants to the right height.

The tiny blue flowers of the water forget-me-not attract bees and butterflies. Ideally your pond should be situated in half sun and half shade.

8. Fill with water until it comes about 5cm (2in) over the gravel of the planting baskets. At this stage you can add a few bunches of oxygenating weeds. Tie each bunch to a stone and let the stone sink to the bottom.

AFTERCARE & TIPS

Keep your pond water topped up in summer. If you have sunk your barrel into the ground, make sure there is an escape route in case any small mammals happen to fall in. A rock or a roof tile emerging from the water is ideal.

LITTLE LABORATORY

Johan Rooms lives in a rented home in Kichijoji, western Tokyo. With no scope to make structural changes to the house or to its wild, uncultivated garden, Johan has pursued his passion for urban farming nonetheless, creating raised beds, green walls and vertical planters in every available patch of space.

Johan is a polymath. His curiosity and lifelong interest in learning have brought him expertise in film, semiotics, linguistics and languages. And as a digital strategist for an e-commerce company, he's similarly adept at computers. But he's never been about gardening. Not until Fukushima.

'When the Fukushima nuclear disaster happened, the city supply lines were struck and the tap water turned radioactive,' says the Belgian, who moved to Tokyo over a decade ago. 'As I have small children, I began thinking about how to do things by myself. I didn't have a clue but I cleared a bit of ground and began learning.'

Johan's garden is dark, north-facing and receives just a few hours light a day. Old plum and maple trees and a labyrinth of ground foliage are the remains of a traditional Japanese garden. They cover old stone pathways that lead to nowhere.

This garden of experimentation has been improvised on a rented property, where it isn't possible to make changes to the landscape.

Unable to start afresh, Johan built himself two 2m² (23ft²) raised beds, positioned them in the sunniest spot in the garden, and plonked a few plug plants in the earth. The first year, most of it failed. By the second year, he had set up the Urban Farming Tokyo Facebook group, a forum for keen enthusiasts, where members share their experiences of growing.

His rapid ascent from novice, he says, was coming to understand the importance of the soil: if it is healthy and well, so your plants will be the same and if not, then good luck.

'At first I was just sticking things in the ground, watering them and expecting them to thrive,' he recalls. 'But then I realised that not only did I have a space and a light problem, I had a soil problem, too.'

Inspired by the 'Do Nothing' method of famed Japanese farmer, Masanobu Fukuoka, who advocated that soil is best cared for without machines, chemicals or extensive weeding, Johan became fascinated with the idea that nature is the soil's perfect caretaker. So he started creating compost with dead leaves from the nearby park. Then he mixed it with coffee grounds, a form of organic matter, and used it to improve the soil structure and its fertility.

'Lots of people push the self-sufficiency agenda, but I'd need too much space to feed my family. However gardening on a small scale like this gives kids a taste of what home-grown produce tastes like, and that way they'll gain respect for farmers,' says Johan.

'The more I read the more I realised that the soil is like a plant. It needs oxygen, nutrition and water. The worms need to eat, and that process releases nutrients back. Organic matter is essential,' says Johan, who allows spent roots to decompose rather than digging them up at the season's end.

'I found that the soil I disturbed by cultivation lost moisture and structure, whereas the soil I didn't interfere with was much healthier and more productive,' he explains.

Johan's family of five now enjoys harvests of tomatoes, cucumbers, lettuces, kale, leeks, cauliflowers and broccoli from the raised beds, as well as rosemary, thyme, lemon balm, lavender, mint and Japanese basil (known as *shiso*) plucked from planters.

To overcome his problem of having barely any ground space, he's installed his own design, a towered, vertical growing system made out of recyclable PET bottles strapped to a wooden pallet.

He has created a vertical PET bottle tower that has a water reservoir for each plant at each level. Wicks in the planted bottles suck up water from their reservoirs. 'This means the plant always has a perfect level of moisture and you can leave it unattended for a week.' The planters installed in the garden today are among 50 home-made prototypes.

Other small-space experiments include a 9m² (100ft²) 'green screen' that he's created by hanging a net above planters full of climbing species like Hechima sponge cucumbers, gourds and goya (bitter melons).

One of his inventions, however, did not prove so useful. Tech-savvy Johan built a modular plant-shaped 'sensor stick' with an Arduino microcontroller inside that is programmed to message Johan with updates on conditions in the garden.

'It reads the amount of sunlight, temperature, moisture in the soil and humidity in the air, and tweets me the results. My idea was to connect it all up to an automatic sprinkler,' he says and, laughing, picks up a small watering can in the shape of an elephant. 'Then I realised that all I needed to do to be smart was use my own senses and this,' he says, waving the can around.

'You don't need to be a Silicon Valley entrepreneur to make gardening work.'

'Vertical planters are a great way of creating farming space out of thin air,' says Johan, who designed his own vertical planting system. 'All you need is a small corner.'

MOONLIT MAGIC

Yoshiko Kuge is an artist and teacher who has been living and working from a studio in the district of Suginami, western Tokyo, for 15 years. Not being a committed gardener, the small, dark yard out back was once a place for mosquitoes, weeds and a washing line until her son-in-law gifted her a small ficus plant. Determined to keep it alive, she began to care for it and then, little by little, to nurture the ground around it.

Yoshiko is a night owl and when the moon is full, she puts down her artist's tools and steps into the back yard to bask in its light. The last weeks of winter, when she senses spring's sap rising, are her favourite time to be in the garden.

Her plants look their best in the moonlit yard, when the ice whites of her flowers illuminate and shimmer: *Kerria Japonica* 'White Cloud', the shuttlecock-like flora of *Hydrangea quercifolia* Snowflake ('Brido'), and the bashful bowl-shaped heads of *Helleborus niger*.

A *Nandina domestica* is also a creature of the dark. Its heavenly, magical properties – according to folklore in these parts – give this elegant shrub the power to dispel bad dreams. It is often planted near doorways in Japan, should you wake from sleep and wish to share your nightmares with it.

When daylight breaks, solitude gives way to sociability. As a tiny garden that mosquitoes like to haunt, it is still not a place in which to entertain. But an old cherry tree, which bears baskets of sour, acidic fruit come summer, allows Yoshiko to share the peculiar magic of her garden with others.

Texture is one way to increase the aesthetic appeal of your garden. The combination of coarse, medium and fine foliage (opposite, left) makes a pleasing composition. Coarse leaves demand attention while small leaves create the illusion of space.

White flowers illuminate a dark space and give a garden a magical feel in the evening. Pale petals are a draw for moths.

'Gardening makes me happy,' says Yoshiko. 'In art you can mostly control what happens. But in a garden you mostly can't.'

Prunus cerasus cherries are perfect for cooking and make a delicious jam that Yoshiko gives to her students, family and friends. Maple leaves picked from the garden delicately line a dish of home-made candied orange peel served with cheesecake.

It is part of the dialogue of sharing between nature and the artist that feeds Yoshiko's spirit. A hydrangea leaf becomes the motif for a handmade ceramic. The undersides of foliage are where she watches caterpillars cocoon themselves in chrysalises and emerge as butterflies.

'She believes in talking to the plants,' says her son Shu. 'I tell her the talking is unnecessary but she says the plants encourage her and she encourages them. I have to admit her air plant flowered this year. Mine has never done that,' he laughs.

WORDS BY LUCY ANNA SCOTT

Lucy Anna Scott is a writer with an artistic interest in stories that explore how plants, trees and landscapes help us better understand ourselves. She co-creates *Lost in London*, an indie magazine that explores the city's wild landscapes. Her other creative non-fiction, informed by her RHS horticultural training at Capel Manor College, has been featured by the Royal Botanic Gardens at Kew, and by *Monocle* and *The Ecologist* among other titles. Her first book, *Lost in London: adventures in the city's wild outdoors*, was published by Portico in 2013.

PHOTOGRAPHY BY JON CARDWELL

Jon Cardwell works extensively for magazines and commercial clients. When he is not on assignment, he spends his time working on personal projects such as photographing modern-day gold miners in Colorado, a football-mad town in the mountains of Guatemala and winter swimmers in the freezing waters of a Finnish river. He lives in south London, where he occasionally gardens.

HOW TOs BY LUCY CONOCHIE

Lucy Conochie is a garden designer, artist and gardener whose portfolio includes a range of urban and rural garden projects, and numerous art exhibitions around the UK. She runs her fast-growing practice, Lucy Conochie Design, from her studio at home in London. Passionate about increasing the range of diverse habitats available for wildlife, she is currently developing perennial wildflower meadows in Suffolk and Dorset.

SOURCES

Eden Gardens
Award-winning garden and horticultural centre that runs courses and community projects
307 Lane Cove Road, Macquarie Park, NSW 2113, Australia
www.edengardens.com/au

Fine Mesh Metals
Industrial metal mesh suppliers, including gabions
www.finemeshmetals.co.uk

Flora Grubb Gardens
Garden centre offering unique plants, décor, pottery, and plant experts
1634 Jerrold Ave, San Francisco, CA 94124
www.floragrubb.com

Greenwood Bonsai Studio
British bonsai centre
www.bonsai.co.uk

Marshalls Seeds
Providing quality seeds, bulbs and plug plants
www.marshalls-seeds.co.uk

Natty Garden
Brooklyn-based garden store with a small selection of plants, shrubs, soil and pots
636 Washington Avenue, Brooklyn, NY 11238
www.nattygarden.com

Prinzessinnengarten
Urban farm dedicated to promoting sustainable living and growing vegetables
Prinzenstrasse 35 – 38, 10969 Berlin, Germany
www.prinzessinnengarten.net

Scotsdales Garden Centre
Independent garden centre
www.scotsdalegardencentre.co.uk

Suttons Seeds
Providing quality seeds, bulbs and plug plants
www.suttons.co.uk

Wholesale Tropicals
Specialist tropical aquatics centre, East London
www.wholesaletropicalsaquatics.co.uk

Wildwoods Water Gardens
Aquatics centre, North London
www.wildwoods.co.uk

Wright & Doyle
Garden workwear unisex clothing, pots & stands, macramé plant hangers
Momosan's Shop, 79a Wilton Way, E8 1BG

Wyevale Garden Centres
Garden centres all over the UK
www.wyevalegardencentres.co.uk